SCIENTISTS WHO FIND GOD

# SCIENTISTS WHO FIND GOD

edited by

## Eric C. Barrett

SLAVIC GOSPEL ASSOCIATION
(BRITISH SECTION) LTD.
Eastbourne, East Sussex BN21 1HF, UK

ISBN 0 9518395 1 9

All Scripture quotations in this book, except those noted otherwise, are
from the New International Version, Copyright © 1973, 1978, 1984 by
New York International Bible Society, and are used by permission.

Design and word-processing: Gillian M. Barrett
Cover design: Nuprint Ltd.

Printed in Great Britain for
SLAVIC GOSPEL ASSOCIATION (BRITISH SECTION)
37A The Goffs, Eastbourne, East Sussex BN21 1HF
by Nuprint Ltd., Harpenden, Herts. AL5 4SE.

# CONTENTS

# FOREWORD

Radio is arguably still the most effective and economic medium for Christian communication. In the later decades of the global communist empire, Slavic Gospel Association used radio to particularly great effect, both to encourage existing Believers, and to share news of God's love with Unbelievers, in Slavic countries. In these nations, church life was difficult, and traditional missionary work dangerous - in some areas it was virtually impossible.

Dr. Eric Barrett, with his wife Gillian, have been volunteer workers with SGA/England since 1967. Also a respected university professor and an internationally-recognised scientist, Dr. Barrett was the obvious choice by SGA to develop a science-based evangelistic radio programme for broadcast across the USSR and elsewhere, as well as related books and audiovisuals. In 1977, SGA's *"Radio Academy of Science"* *(RADAS)* program came into being. Its 30-minute magazine-style format was designed to uproot weeds of scientific atheism from the minds of well-educated listeners, and to plant the Gospel of Jesus Christ in their place.

The RADAS project has been greatly blessed of God. From 1980 to 1992, Dr. Barrett and others in SGA's Radio Division in Wheaton, Illinois, produced hundreds of RADAS programs. Each one was broadcast repeatedly from different short-wave radio stations to many regions of the USSR. RADAS has helped many people spiritually, and I am sure it also contributed to the debate against the atheism and materialism so rampant in communist societies. The outcome of this debate has been sweeping changes in government, and prevalent attitudes toward the church, in many countries. Christian radio stations have now been established within many such areas, and RADAS programs are being re-aired on medium wave and FM stations inside Russia, Belarus, Ukraine and elsewhere.

I am glad that these programs, which were so carefully and painstakingly prepared, are also being used in other ways to minister to Christians and non-Christians throughout the world. This book, like its valued predecessor *"Scientists Who Believe"* (© Moody Press in 1984) is one result.

I recommend *"Scientists Who Find God"* especially to Christians who need to defend their faith in the face of growing apathy and agnosticism. I also recommend it to non-Christians who are increasingly dissatisfied with atheism, agnosticism and the so-called New Age. The experiences of its contributors will strike many chords in the hearts and minds of its readers.

The apostle Paul warned Timothy in 2 Timothy 3:5-7 that he should avoid the influences of men who are *"always learning and never able to come to the knowledge of the truth."* This is a book about scientists who, through the grace of God, have come to the knowledge of the truth and it has made them free (John 8:31-32). They have shared their experiences with Dr. Eric Barrett so that he can pass them on to you. May God bless you beyond measure as you learn how His beloved Son, Jesus Christ, is building His church around the world.... even in the world of Science!

*Dr. Robert W. Provost*
*President*
*Slavic Gospel Association*
*Loves Park*
*Illinois*
*USA.*

# PREFACE

In Science, as in Economics, *forecasting* is notoriously difficult. Combine those two fields of enquiry - as in publishing books with scientific themes - and forecasting success may be virtually impossible! Certainly I have to confess that I did not foresee that, of the 20 or so books I have written or edited, the most successful to date (judged by numbers of reprints, copies sold, and translations involved) would prove to be *"Scientists Who Believe"* (with David Fisher), first published by Moody Press, Chicago in 1984.

Looking back, one reason would suggest that *"Scientists Who Believe"* was such a success because it addressed not just one branch of Science, but much of it. But I believe the foremost reason by far has been that it set out to debate some of today's most fascinating and important questions, involving not only Science, but also the Christian faith. The questions included these:

- Are Science and the Christian faith mutually exclusive, in conflict with each other or, perhaps, complementary - providing different perspectives on truths of the Universe, and life on Earth?
- Can Scientists honestly and justifiably believe in a Supreme Being, who created everything from nothing?
- Can Christians study Science without threat to their faith in God?
- Is it possible to pursue a career in Science, and practice Christianity, without compromising either?

Today, interest in these questions is arguably greater than ever before. Thus, both in response to popular demand, and because I am sure that personal experiences are particularly helpful in answering the kinds of questions listed above, I have agreed to prepare a companion volume to *"Scientists Who Believe"*. This new book, like its predecessor, is based almost exclusively on scripts prepared originally for use in Slavic Gospel Association's 'RADAS' (Radio Academy of Science) broadcasts. As in *"Scientists Who Believe"* the contributors come from many countries of the world, and from many fields of scientific research and application. However, recognising that the 'Pacific rim' is fast becoming the world's number one growth area in Science and Technology, a higher proportion (over one-third) of the contributors in *"Scientists Who Find God"* have strong connections with that area. And, reflecting parallel trends towards more informality in life in general, and more discursive styles of presentation in the RADAS programme in recent years, more chapters (about one-half) in this new book are presented in dialogue form.

Where appropriate and possible, the original RADAS script materials have been updated to take account of any recent changes in the personal situations of the people involved, and/or developments in their scientific and spiritual insights. In a few cases, however, despite often lengthy enquiries, such up-dating has not been possible because some colleagues have moved both work and home, and have been impossible to trace! If they discover they are featured here, I hope they will want to contact me, not only so that new printings may, if necessary, be updated in their cases too, but so that I can send them the complimentary copies of this book which they so richly deserve! In the meantime, I am glad of this opportunity to warmly thank all my contributors for the willingness they have expressed - earlier, or more recently - to share their personal beliefs and experiences with many through the RADAS project. In two cases (Gitt and Murakami), chapters have been prepared from material originally published in the German and Japanese language versions respectively of *"Scientists Who Believe";* and in one case (Chaplar), a personal story written recently in English has been included ahead of its use in radio. My thanks are due to these three friends, too.

I would also like to thank the following for their assistance in many different ways: my present and former colleagues in the Slavic Gospel Association for all their friendship and help over many years; my wife Gillian and children Andrew and Stella for their love, encouragement and understanding through very busy and demanding times; my wife Gillian (deservedly getting a special second mention!) for many hours on the word processor preparing radio scripts and related manuscripts, including the camera-ready copy for this book; and, of course, all those others who have so unselfishly shared their personal stories and revelations through RADAS during the last 15 years, but whose testimonies it has not been possible to include this time. All these wonderful folk have warmed and enriched my life, have brought spiritual blessings to many of our listeners and readers, and, above all, have greatly honoured God.

I pray and trust that this new book will be used of God through helping many more scientists - and others - find Him too.

*Eric C. Barrett, Backwell, North Somerset, UK.*          *November 1996*

# 1.

# THE FAITH OF THINKING PEOPLE

**Drs. Michael and Ruth Gaylor**
*(Visiting Professors, Bogar Agricultural University, Indonesia)*

*Even today, the degree of Doctor of Philosophy is a relatively rare academic distinction, much less common than Bachelor or Master degrees. Thus, it is rare indeed to find a husband and wife who both hold Ph.Ds. Yet this is the case with* **Dr. Michael Gaylor** *and his wife* **Dr. Ruth Gaylor.** *Originally both graduates of Geography from the University of Southampton in the United Kingdom, Michael went on to specialise in Geomorphology (the science of landforms), and Ruth in Climatology (study of climate, and one of the specialisms of the Editor). Indeed, it was because of a common interest in Climatology that Ruth and Dr. Barrett first corresponded, and later met. This led in time to the preparation of the RADAS radio script on which this Chapter is based.*

*Correspondence between the Gaylors and Dr. Barrett has, however, usually been over very long distances: in the early 1980s Michael and Ruth worked as Associate Professors in the University of Calgary, Alberta, Canada; after this, they relocated to Indonesia, to serve as Visiting Professors in the Bogar Agricultural University. In Indonesia they have also been actively involved in the life of local Christian churches.*

*An important stimulus to people thinking about religious faiths in Indonesia was the national government's edict in 1966 that everyone in that country should register affiliation to one religious faith, and give their loyalty to only one god. One result of this edict has been, as Michael and Ruth have described it, a* "very exciting period for the local churches". *Christianity has blossomed in Indonesia, particularly amongst the more intellectual and better educated sections of society, for it is becoming increasingly* "the faith of thinking people."

----

Editor:    Michael and Ruth, you have both led more than usually varied and interesting lives as researchers and professors in the broad field of the environmental sciences, working first in Europe, then in North America, and most recently in South-east Asia. Because of constraints of space and time, we will have to focus on only one of these areas today - so let us choose South-east Asia, where you are working now.
           Please tell us where you are based, and a little about your present academic responsibilities.

Ruth:      You are right about our global nomadism! After training in England, Michael and I were both Assistant Professors in Canada for a number of years, but then we moved from the centre of a northern continent to an island virtually on the equator. That was quite a startling change for us! However, we have now made most of the necessary personal adjustments. At present we are working as Visiting Professors in an agricultural university on the island of Java. We are helping to develop undergraduate curricula, as well as applied research programmes, in our respective areas of expertise.

Michael:   My work is in the Soils Department of Bogar University. As you would expect in an agricultural college, the Soils Department is a large one. It has 32 members on its academic faculty. We teach a wide range of topics - soil classification, soil chemistry, remote sensing, soil erosion and conservation, and others too.

Editor:    I am specially interested myself in remote sensing - the 'Science of observation from a distance'. Tell us about some of the research projects in which you have been involved in this field.

Michael: One topic I researched for the government used remote sensing to survey areas of Sumatra earmarked for population resettlement, in this case through the interpretation of air-photos and Landsat satellite images. The Indonesian Government Department of Transmigration intended to move people from Java, which is very overcrowded, to sparsely populated areas on other islands. Some of the selected areas in eastern Sumatra were so sparsely populated they were no more than little-explored virgin jungle. We used remote sensing imagery to map these areas in detail. Sites for new towns and villages were selected as a result of our analyses, and then the areas were cleared for building.

Editor: Was it difficult to obtain suitable satellite images for these purposes?

Michael: At first the biggest problem was the delay in getting the data. Indonesia had no receiving station capable of receiving images directly from the Landsat satellites themselves. So the main Earth Resources Observation System (EROS) Data Center, at Sioux Falls, South Dakota in the United States, would have to send us the data, recorded on magnetic tape, and our computers would then translate the raw data into map images.

More recently, Indonesia has built its own Landsat Receiving Station, actually on Java. This type of satellite passes overhead every 18 days, and we now receive new images from space, instantly, by radio.

Editor: To be able to obtain images quite often must be particularly important in such a cloudy region as Indonesia.

Michael: Exactly! As you know Landsat carries only visible and infrared sensors, so it cannot see through clouds. Having access to frequently-repeated observations greatly increases our opportunities of collecting information even from areas that are often covered by clouds.

Editor: In the meantime, Ruth, I believe you have overseen the setting up of a wholly new department in the same University?

Ruth: Yes, my main task has been to establish the Department of Climatology. This now has 10 academic staff - and provides courses for over 1400 students every year! Most students in the college are required to study basic climatology, and about 35 each year study climate as their speciality, or 'major' discipline.

Editor:    Michael, have you been involved in any new teaching projects too?

Michael: Yes, I have. Indeed, in Timor, an island in eastern Indonesia, I have helped to organize a whole new Environmental Studies Centre. Apart from lecture courses studying the theory of the environment, we have organized some practical training courses too. The first of these involved planning the reclamation of some derelict land. In fact, this kind of applied study is a valuable exercise for both students and staff alike!

Editor:    What kind of impact does this sort of study have on the local native population?

Michael: A very positive one, I hope. For example, we like these exercises to be profitable for the local farmers. We want them to see the kinds of things they could do themselves to increase the areas of productive cultivated land.

Editor:    It is clear from all you say that Indonesia is obviously a very interesting, but challenging, place in which to work!

Michael: It certainly is! In some ways it's a typical Developing Country, faced by many problems. But it is really exciting to see advances taking place with respect to key activities including farming, fishing, and general use of the land.

However, in some other ways, Indonesia is a very *unusual* country indeed.

Editor:    Very unusual? What have you in mind particularly?

Michael: Well, we live in an age which has seen many people - even whole nations - renouncing religious beliefs. We have even seen many governments discouraging religion, certainly not actively encouraging it! But, in the mid-1960s, the Government of Indonesia decreed that everyone should register affiliation to a particular religion - and believe in only ONE god!

Editor:    You are right! That is a highly unusual thing to have been decreed! I do not think I have heard of such an edict in any other country in recent times. But would not a law like that be likely to increase nominal, rather than genuine, religious beliefs?

Michael: Yes, and to some degree I am sure it has. People who previously did not believe in any god at all found they had to become associated with a named religion. And others, who had had only a hazy faith, in some cases in many gods, had to choose a new religion which believes in a *single* god. One faith which believes in one god is Islam. This has long been well-represented in southeast Asia. Where we live in western Java, it has become so well-established that most aspects of life and culture are related to it. Not surprisingly, since the government edict in 1966 the Moslem sector of the population has grown....

Ruth: ....But proportionately, the Christian faith has shown an even bigger growth! And many people who chose to join the Christian church out of necessity in 1966 have subsequently become convinced that it is a faith which really works.

Editor: This whole situation you describe is quite fascinating! Although there must also be many folk in Indonesia who previously held religious beliefs purely out of superstition or tradition, the new law you have described must have made even people like that think more carefully than they would otherwise have done about what they might best believe, and why. Perhaps many folk have even been encouraged to compare the respective merits of different faiths?

Michael: They have indeed! And Ruth and I have found that this has been especially true in colleges and universities.

Editor: Some people might find that surprising, and say "*Aren't well-educated staff and students the LAST people to think seriously about religion?*"

Michael: Well, in our experience they certainly are not! We find well-educated people to be the very ones who think most actively about themselves.... who they are, where they are going.... what life is really all about.

Editor: You suggested just now that it is the Christian churches which are growing particularly quickly. Can you suggest why this is so?

Ruth: We have wondered about this a lot. We have come to rationalise it in three ways.

The *first* conclusion we have reached is that Christianity seems to us to be the only faith which provides a fully satisfactory philosophical perspective of life: Christianity has a unified view of all areas of human experience. Simple, uneducated folk can appreciate its basic teachings, but well-educated people can find complete satisfaction in it too, on higher intellectual planes. Personally I think that there is an important difference between Christianity and some other faiths in this respect. Some religions are religions of acceptance without questioning: they relieve the individual of any responsibility to think through God's role, or their own, in the world. Christianity, though, is rapidly becoming the *faith of thinking people* in Indonesia, probably because the Bible teaches that every Christian Believer must work out the implications of his or her own faith in the context of their own everyday life and conduct. Now this may be a difficult process for some, but is very satisfying for the intellectual.

The *second* conclusion we have reached is that Christianity is built on a personal knowledge of God: people can actually experience and enjoy a one-to-one relationship with the One they worship. We have discovered that, in some other faiths, the standards set for people to strive for are unattainable: their gods cannot, or will not, help the Believer to become perfect, maybe because these conceptualize God as one who is too high and holy.... One who is far off, even disinterested in human affairs. The individual Believer may try to gain God's favour, but has to do so by his or her own good works! Not surprisingly, people who follow such faiths can never be sure that their lives are good enough to prove acceptable to their gods.

By contrast, the Christian message to the world is truly *wonderful*. It is that we do not begin by earning God's favour: God wants to give HIS favour to US! Neither do we win it by good deeds; but we can receive His favour as a free gift. For this we must first believe He is real, then ask Him to forgive our past misdeeds. It is then He can begin to give us His love and help, remoulding our lives, right here and now, until they are truly acceptable to Him. This sounds almost too good to be true - but it is exactly what He has promised to do.

And I would like to add a *third* reason why the Christian faith is spreading so fast in Indonesia. It is because the followers of Christ themselves are such good advertisements for it! Among the truly dedicated Christians - those who really know Him, as distinct from those nominal Christians who just practice some empty ritual - there is a joy, a warmth of friendliness, and a real spiritual power that is evident nowhere else in Indonesian society. Christians are different, their faith obviously works! That is why so many other people are wanting to test Christianity for themselves.

Editor:    I have heard it said that some people have joined the Christian churches in Indonesia because this is becoming 'fashionable'. What have you to say about this?

Michael: I am afraid it is true in some cases. However, there is a natural deterrent: for many new Christians, life becomes harder, not easier, sometimes becoming even very difficult indeed! Let me tell you about one young fellow who found God through a vibrant faith in Jesus Christ. First he was rejected by his wife, who strongly held different beliefs; then he was thrown out of his home by her family. Then he was wrongly accused of certain crimes, convicted on false evidence, and sent to jail. This would have been a real test of *any* man's faith! But our friend came through it all remarkably. In this way it was obvious to others that God was with him. His faith was actually strengthened in prison - not least because he had the time there to study it in detail. Now released, he is a most effective Christian worker, praising God for being faithful to him through all his difficulties.

Editor:    Michael and Ruth, there is the opportunity for just one more question: is there any danger that students who come to find God through faith in Jesus Christ may become just INTELLECTUAL Christians? You spoke of Christianity as.... what were your words?.... the *"faith of thinking people"*. Not all thinkers are very PRACTICAL people, are they?

Michael: No, indeed they are not. And I, myself am aware of a number of simple, practical, things which an academic like me cannot do. But, remember, we also said that Christianity has a unified view of all human experience. True Christianity cannot be restricted to mere intellectual activity, or locked up in a church building, or confined to a short performance of some ritual now and then. Ruth and I consider that our most important responsibility is to encourage Christian graduates to see their future careers as spheres in which they are specially called to serve God in practical ways. Each true Christian believes that God directs his activities, for God has a special place, a unique type of service or ministry, if you prefer to call it this, for each of His followers. This being true, every new graduate must see his or her career as a special channel through which it is possible to serve God, and his or her home and work-place as areas in which to serve the local church. University graduates are still relatively rare in Indonesia. Educated people like these have vital parts to play in the growth of the Christian faith. They must be prepared to be the leaders of local church congregations!

So in summary, each Christian benefits greatly from faith in God but, in return, God expects all Christian Believers to surrender their lives to Him, so that His own plans for the world can be achieved through them.

Editor: Michael and Ruth, thank you for sharing all these things with us today. You have given us so much to think about.

I will try to summarise. It has been suggested that Christianity is *"the faith of thinking people"*; that *"Christianity has a unified view of all areas of human experience"*; and that *"Christians are different! Their faith obviously works! Other people are wanting to test it for themselves!"*

So here is a fascinating question for you, our reader. Suppose for a moment YOUR government passed a new law, insisting that you must personally accept one religious faith, albeit of your own choice! Which would YOU choose....?

In many religions, men and women have to perfect themselves. But, if everyone is naturally imperfect already, this is both philosophically and practically impossible. We cannot perfect ourselves any more than, say, a broken down clock can make itself tell the time again.

Drs. Michael and Ruth Gaylor have confirmed that

Christianity does not encounter such a difficulty. Jesus Christ does not ask us to perfect ourselves so that we might gain His acceptance. Rather, God promises to help us towards perfection, by giving us of His own strength and wisdom: this is His favour to us. Christianity is built on finding God, and developing a close personal relationship with Him.

So, the message of Christianity is simple, yet very profound and practical: this loving, caring God is willing to enter and repair our lives right here and now. Read the other chapters in this book, then make your choice: why not choose to find God, love Him, and follow Him?

# 2.

# APPROACHING THE BIBLE WITH AN OPEN MIND

### Dr. Roy Spencer

*(Senior Scientist, Marshall Space Flight Center, Huntsville, Alabama, USA)*

**Dr. Roy Spencer** *is a top scientist with NASA, the world-famous National Aeronautics and Space Administration of the USA: the organisation which has been responsible - amongst many other things - for sending men to the Moon. Although based at the Marshall Space Flight Center in Huntsville, Alabama, Roy's own scientific responsibilities and interests are relatively local, lying mainly in the development of new sensors for Earth observation and monitoring, particularly in the microwave (1 mm to 1 cm radiation wavelength) region of the electromagnetic spectrum.*

*It was because of these interests that the Editor first met Roy, for some of Dr. Barrett's professional concerns overlap strongly into the same areas of environmental science. Indeed, for several years, Dr. Spencer carried technical management responsibilities for work undertaken by the Editor and his staff in the University of Bristol, England for NASA, based on data from an American satellite family's passive microwave imaging instrument, the 'Special Sensor Microwave Imager' (SSM/I).*

*Thus, the Editor has come to know Roy and his family well, and has a very high regard for Roy's scientific studies. However, even Dr. Barrett was surprised recently to see him being interviewed on BBC-TV on results of new research, just published by Dr. Spencer and a colleague, on the topic of possible 'global warming' trends in the Earth's atmosphere! But this was not all. Because the results of that research were considered so important, the next day Dr. Spencer was summoned to the White House in Washington, DC to brief advisers to the US President on their findings - and how they should be interpreted. One reason why this was necessary, Roy thinks, is because some elements of the mass media not only sensationalised, but also misinterpreted that work - in some cases clearly without having read the relevant research report!*

*Roy has been philosophical about this, freely admitting that this happens often, not only with key writings in science, but in other areas of life also. Indeed, he confesses that he himself used to dismiss the Christian faith without having read the Bible, and used to discount the Bible as a book of great worth without having properly considered its message.... all because he made the wrong initial assumptions about them both!*

--------

Editor:   Dr. Roy Spencer, we will want to learn something of your scientific research.... but first I would like to ask you about your personal life because, having known you for many years, I know it underwent an important change when you became a Christian. We will be interested to learn how this change came about. So, tell us, what was your attitude toward Christianity before you became a Christian?

Roy:   To be honest, what little I knew about Christianity *bothered* me! In particular, Christians in my area who went from house to house inviting people to events at their churches *irritated* me! These people clearly believed they were part of the one, true religion, if indeed there was one. I asked myself, how could they be so sure of this? If Christianity were true, then would not most people in the world be Christians? And since they are not, how could anyone in good conscience devote his or her life to any such philosophy

without at least investigating all other world religions too? At
that time I had a fundamental difficulty with the Bible. Was
not its first book, Genesis, believed by many to be false.... a
myth.... and therefore not a true account of how the Universe
and life came into being? Based on the little evidence at my
disposal it seemed to me that Christians picked and chose
what they wanted to believe, selecting some things in the
Bible, while rejecting others, often quite arbitrarily. How,
then, could I regard it as what it claims to be, the inspired
Word of God? Surely, I thought, if there really was a God
who had infinite power and wisdom, He would protect His
inspired Word against any errors of interpretation?

Editor:   Having so many doubts about the Bible, what eventually
made you willing to read it?

Roy:      Several things!
Probably the most important involved my scientific research,
so perhaps I should say something about this now. Scientists
say they are *objective* in their work. However, I am often
disturbed by the attitude some of my fellow scientists take.
They often seem to be more interested in advancing their
careers, or maintaining their jobs, or protecting a pet theory,
than in searching for truth!
In this regard I came to realize that many scientists put too
much trust in their *assumptions*. Just about any science
problem involves assumptions. Indeed, they are usually
necessary to make problems easier to solve. Unfortunately,
once assumptions have been made, scientists often forget the
possibility that those assumptions might just have been
wrong!
Personally I have long been interested in satellite
observations of naturally upwelling radiation in the
microwave region of the electromagnetic spectrum. Such
data are useful for monitoring many features of the Earth's
atmosphere and surface. Like you, one of my chief interests
has been in the possibility of using these data for monitoring
global rainfall. However, for a time everyone else assumed
that microwave observations would be of no use for
monitoring rainfall over land, because they thought ice
particles, higher in the clouds than raindrops, could not be

transparent at microwave wavelengths.  So they thought that the ice particles between the satellites and the raindrops we were trying to observe would block the radiation we wished to monitor, producing erroneous results.  I spent several years trying to get the scientific community to accept some results of mine that showed that this was a wrong assumption.  I ran into so much opposition that I realised that scientists, as a group, are not much more objective than anyone else!

A second example of this has been more recent, and in many ways much more public.  This involves a recent paper I wrote with my colleague, Dr. John Christy of NASA.  It was entitled *"Precise monitoring of global temperature trends from satellites"*, and was published in the American journal *"Science"*....

Editor:  ....Stories on which were immediately run by newspapers, radio and TV in many countries of the world - including the UK, where I watched you on BBC Television News!  I would have to say, though, Roy, that your paper not only surprised, but even disappointed, many people!  As you know well, most recent research on climate change seems to have suggested that, on average, global temperatures have been rising recently, and that *human activities* may be largely to blame.  Then came your paper in *"Science"*.  At the end of your analysis of satellite microwave data, you dropped the quiet bombshell that these data had revealed, and here I quote, *"....no obvious long-term global temperature trend"*!  This conclusion startled many people!  Did it surprise *you*?

Roy:  No, it did not - although this may have been because John and I tried to analyse the data without any preconceived ideas as to what the results should be.  Our aim was not to provide evidence for, or against, global warming - but to determine whether data from satellites could be used to monitor global temperatures and their changes through time.

Editor:  So your results did not surprise you, Roy.  But the media treated them as if they were SENSATIONAL!  Some scientists criticised them strongly - and advisers to the US President wanted your conclusions explained to them in detail - hence your summons to the White House!  Why were there such extreme reactions?

Roy:      I guess the *media* were interested because journalists thought
          our paper was saying something different from usual, even
          something unexpected and controversial. *Presidential
          advisers* thought the paper might be important because
          legislation was pending to limit industrial emissions of
          carbon dioxide - a gas widely blamed for global warming.
          Any such limitation would be very expensive to the US
          economy. So the government wanted to know whether it was
          really necessary.
          As for *scientists*, some were critical because they clearly
          believed we were jeopardising their research funding,
          thinking we were suggesting global warming is not a problem
          after all!

Editor:   Many new scientific papers arouse the interest of at least
          some of their readers. Quite a few papers manage to be at
          least mildly controversial. But not many are so openly and
          publicly criticised as yours. Do you consider that, in the case
          of your paper, the criticisms were fair?

Roy:      No, Dr. Christy and I thought most of them were *not* fair.
          Some of the critics obviously had not read our paper
          themselves. Others clearly had not understood it. Many
          critics did not criticise it honestly. For example, they
          suggested that we had said global warming was not a
          problem. Some made our statement on past trends sound like
          a prediction of future trends, which it was not.

Editor:   Well, Roy, I certainly have read your paper myself, and I
          think it is admirably concise and clear! It confirms that we
          now have an excellent satellite data set for evaluating
          temperatures on a global scale, and at various altitudes in the
          atmosphere. Indeed, in many ways the satellite data are far
          superior to data from thermometers on the ground, or within
          the atmosphere itself, for these suffer from many unhelpful
          influences. And your paper indicates that, whilst you found
          global temperatures to have fluctuated greatly over time
          periods ranging from weeks to several years, there was, to
          quote you *"No obvious trend over the 10-year period"* of
          your study.

Roy:      Precisely, Eric! And that is why much criticism of the paper
          was so inappropriate! We did not say global warming has not

taken place - nor that it will not do so unless we manage the planet more sensitively. We simply said that no general temperature trend could be identified through the rather brief period we studied. And that is a very different thing!

But let me return to your questions about Christianity, and the Bible. The time came when I began to realise, to my initial surprise, that there was a group of scientists who believed that the Universe and all life in it were actually created by some greater intelligent Being. I became interested in these beliefs, for it is a general assumption by many that both the Universe, and all life in it, have come about by chance. Could this be another example of a wrong assumption, I wondered? I began to find it interesting that the arguments put forward by those who proposed the Universe had not evolved spontaneously, but had been created, were *entirely scientific* arguments! So I began to study their case very carefully. After some months of study and analysis I finally became convinced that the theory of creation had a much better scientific basis than the theory of evolution: the creation model was better able to explain the physical and biological complexity in the world today than the evolution model. What *really* intrigued me was the possibility that, after all I had thought previously, Genesis, the first book of the Bible - might indeed be true! This realization led me to open a Bible for the first time, and to read it for myself, from its beginning.

But a second important reason why I became open to reading the Bible was that I had a very intelligent friend who clearly believed all that was told in the Bible. My family and I accepted this friend's invitation to accompany him to church one Sunday. There, I was amazed by the genuine concern and friendliness shown by many of the people. So, my friend's intelligence, and the friendliness of the folk at his church, also helped to change my attitude toward Christianity. Clearly this was not a faith confined to simple, or socially maladjusted, people as I had once thought.

Editor:     And so you became a convinced creationist before becoming a Christian! That is unusual, and interesting. But tell us, what clinched your decision to become a follower of Jesus

Christ?

Roy:    A whole combination of things.

As I investigated what had been written about other religions, I became aware that many world religions assume evolution to be true. The Bible was the only place where I had read about creation of the material Universe, literally from nothing! The Bible teaches that it was God, who has existed for ever, who created everything.

Next, the work of many historians showed me that the Bible was by far the most accurate and best-substantiated ancient book we have.... both in its portrayal of historical events and places, and the care with which it was copied by the scribes. Also, the contemporary enemies of Jesus, who would have liked to have been able to disprove his divinity, could not deny His many miracles.... for too many people were eye witnesses to what Jesus did. Even the enemies of Jesus were unable to dispute the *fact* of His amazing deeds, only their *source*: they asserted, feebly, that an EVIL superhuman power had done them instead of the GOOD God!

Finally, upon reading the Bible, I was struck by the unity of its message.... the way it agreed with itself even though it was written by many different people, from the wealthiest to the poorest, over a period of many hundreds of years. As I read more of the Bible, I found that its message was not what I had expected; indeed, some of it was quite *contrary* to what I would have liked to believe! But the overwhelming weight of evidence in its favour made me change not only my mind about it, but also my total philosophy of life. I guess this is one meaning of the Biblical concept of 'conversion'....!

I was particularly pleased to discover that the Bible seemed to have been written to satisfy those like me who read it critically, just as much as those who could accept its message on a simpler level. For example, it did not exaggerate when dealing with great events, such as the miracles, but instead presented them factually, without any evidence of our natural human desire to over-dramatise or embellish.

So, at last, I had to face the reality, based on all the evidence, that the tenets of Christianity are true, and that Christianity really changes people for the better. At least as important as this, however, was some intuition within me which seemed to confirm that what I was reading in the Bible must be true!

Thus, my decision to become a Christian involved some faith on my part, but a faith that was well-founded on reasons for believing. I then did as the first century Christians did, by confessing to others that I had become a Christian Believer, and by being baptized. In this regard I understood that *being completely covered* with water symbolized my readiness for Christ to bury my original, evil nature.... and that my *coming out of the water* symbolized Christ raising me to life with a new nature like His own, and with a new ability to live as He wishes.

Editor:  My dictionary tells me that the Hebrew word used in the original Biblical text for 'conversion' means 'turning around'. Clearly, Roy, you have experienced an *intellectual* conversion - in the way you see and understand the Universe.... and also a *spiritual* conversion - based on the way you see and understand God. If so, there must have been related changes in your way of life. What about these?

Roy:  As I have come to know God, the Creator, personally there have been many positive changes, both in my personal life and in the ways I interact with others! Most importantly, I have come to know great inner peace and comfort, for all Christians have the promise of strength and help from the Lord. My new faith has also changed my everyday priorities: the spiritual welfare of others has become more important to me than my own personal comfort. Many members of my family, and my friends and colleagues in NASA, have remarked that I am truly a changed person, more confident and more composed. So it is clear there have been changes in my life - for they have been obvious to other people too.

Editor:  Your emphasis on creation as a major proof of Christianity is very interesting - and probably unusual amongst Christians. Could you explain briefly some of the modern Creationist arguments which support the Biblical claims in this respect?

Roy:  There are so many, it is difficult to know which ones to mention 'briefly'! But a good place to start is with the *origin of the Universe*. The First Law of Thermodynamics states that the total amount of matter and energy is not changing. If this were the only natural law to be satisfied, then it would be possible that the Universe could have existed forever.

However, the Second Law of Thermodynamics states that everything in the Universe is running down. The available energy in the Universe is being degraded into a less useful form. Thus, according to this principle, our Universe is dying. If the Universe were very old, by now it would have experienced what astronomers call a 'heat death'.... in which entropy would be infinite. Since there is no evidence for this, some astronomers have postulated that the Second Law of Thermodynamics must have been reversed some time in the past! But do you remember my earlier comment about scientists' assumptions? The assumption that the Second Law of Thermodynamics has reversed sometime in the past may or may not be true: it falls entirely outside the realm of natural science, of what we currently know about how the Universe works. Indeed, it might even be regarded as *anti*-scientific, since it is the opposite of what is observed.

Partly because of the problems such assumptions pose, there are now new theories of how the Universe got started. A majority of astronomers now agree that the Universe had a beginning. But what do they say caused the Universe to begin? Some say it created itself, literally out of nothing. Surely it is much more logical for us to believe that the Universe was caused by something greater than itself!

A second issue is the *complexity of life*. In recent years, advances in our ability to observe the living cell, and understand how its different components work, have led to the understanding that a living cell is in fact a very intricate machine. The information content within this machine is vast! An increasing number of scientists consider it to be impossible that such a structure could have evolved through random processes, as evolutionists assume.

So, even some prominent evolutionists have now abandoned their theory of the evolution of life - which seems to me to be based on a combination of misinterpretation of the evidence, plus blind faith. Indeed, the probability that the basic unit of life, DNA, could have arisen by chance has been examined in detail, and has been found to be mathematically essentially

ZERO!

Actually, the list of arguments for creation goes on, almost endlessly. And I must point out, that ultimately either creation - or evolution - must be true. There is no third possibility! Basically, everything happened either by accident, or by design. Even the evolutionists and creationists agree on this point! And, remember, the Bible is the only religious book where it is taught that a pre-existing God created everything, out of nothing....

Yet the Bible - the book Christians are certain is the Word of God - is probably the most unfairly criticized publication in the whole of history. Here is a book that has been criticised enormously - though often by people who, like some who criticised our paper on global warming, either have *not read it* or have *not understood it....* or have *not wanted to accept its conclusions*!

Editor: You suggested earlier that some scientists who read your global temperature paper did not want to accept its conclusions because they felt their personal research funding was threatened by it. Perhaps the Bible has a somewhat similar effect on many people: they feel their personal beliefs and ways of life are threatened by its message? Maybe this is even understandable, for the message of the Bible is truly dramatic and unexpected, as you said earlier.

Roy: It certainly is! Yet whether we are talking about progress in science, or trying to head our personal lives in the right direction, I am sure we ought to study the relevant literature *objectively*.

Scientists often fall into the trap of looking for data which suit their hypotheses, instead of looking for truth. Conversely, many people shy away from information which could help them in their everyday lives because it does not fit their preconceived notions, or personal wishes. The productive approach to science is to try to interpret data as honestly as possible, even though the results may be unexpected or unnerving. It is the same with spiritual truths! It took me a long time to approach the Bible with an open mind. But I am very glad there came a time when I did.

Editor: Roy, we have found your arguments, and personal

experiences, most thought-provoking. My last question must
be this: What is your advice to anyone who may still disagree
with your conclusions - scientific, or scriptural?

Roy:     My advice is the same for scientific matters and Biblical
matters alike: do not necessarily believe what other people
tell you is the truth!    FIND OUT FOR YOURSELF!
Establish the assumptions upon which others base their
opinions.    Then try to get information about the opposing
view.    Scientists love to appear as though they have the
answers, when too often they do not, for example in respect
of the origin of life, and of the Universe.    Often their
proposals are ones for which no direct evidence can be found.
No one observed those processes, no one can test their
hypotheses of how they happened, and no one can devise
experiments which would put them to the test!

Unfortunately it is often true that what we learn from others is
based less on evidence, and more on unsubstantiated beliefs.
In relation to the basic claims of Christianity, DO WHAT I
DID!  Read the Bible. Judge this for itself. Put it to the test.
Do this, and I am sure you, too, will find the Bible not only to
be in agreement with proven facts of science - but also to be
the book which will lead you, too, to a personal faith in God.

# 3.

# THE TRUTH THAT MAKES SENSE

**Professor Dr.-Ing. Werner Gitt**
*(Director, Federal Institute of Physics and Technology,
Braunschweig, Germany)*

**Professor Dr.-Ing. Werner Gitt** *is a German scientist who has long been involved in research in the fields of Numerical Mathematics, Cybernetics, and Information Technology. He is the author of numerous original scientific papers in these fields. He stresses, though, that his personal story has more common elements, for example his experience that a busy life - even though it may be relatively successful and superficially problem-free - can divert attention from spiritual needs and opportunities. On the surface, life may seem fine.... but underneath there may be a deep-seated, yet unfulfilled, desire for love, acceptance, or - particularly in the case of intellectuals like Professor Gitt -* fundamental truth!

*Werner Gitt was born in Prussia in 1937. After school and practical work, he studied at the Technical University in Hanover from 1963 to 1968, gaining a degree in Engineering. From 1968 to 1971 he was a research assistant at the Institute of Cybernetics at the Technical University of Aachen. After just two years research he was awarded his doctorate. From 1971 he held a leading post at the Federal Institute of Physics and Technology in Braunschweig (Brunswick), and in 1978 became Director and Professor at that Institute. He is the author of numerous original scientific papers in his personal areas of specialism.*

*Werner met his wife Marion during his student days in Aachen, and they married in 1966. Their son Carsten was born in September 1967, and daughter Rona in April 1969. It was not until after all this that seeds of truth about God, which Werner had received as a child, were watered, germinated, and then began to mature and finally bear fruit in his life.*

*Today, Werner and Marion are glad that their children have grown up well and bring them a lot of joy. Both Carsten and Rona have made their own decisions to follow the path of faith in God, and enjoy being involved at church. Professor Gitt is much occupied in speaking, and writing, about science and the Christian faith.* "Looking back," *he says* "I am astonished at how I have become an author of Christian books without ever wanting to, or suspecting that I might.... but if God opens doors, we should go through them, for what He wishes will be blessed by Him!"

*This Chapter has been adapted from one by Professor Gitt entitled* "Zuverlässige Information" *in the German edition of* "Scientists Who Believe" ("Gewißheit ohne Beweise?"), *which was edited by E.C.Barrett and D. Fisher, and published by Brunnen-Verlag in 1988. Translation of the original from the German was undertaken by Mrs. Hilary Warner.*

---

I was born on 22 February 1937 on my parent's farm in Raineck, East Prussia. My early life was disrupted much by World War II. In October 1944, when I was seven years old, my family fled from Raineck to Peterswalde in south-east Prussia. Then, in January 1945, news of the Russian advance on this region reached us far too late for comfort: panic was heightened by everyone saying *"Get out if you can!"* As I was ill and running a high temperature at that time I remember being carried out of the living room on my bed, and being put on the escape cart whilst still in it! In great haste we fled again, trekking with horse and cart, but were soon overhauled and stopped by the Russians. My brother Fritz, who was then 15 years old, was taken straight off the cart and had to go with them. He never came back. My mother was dragged off to the Ukraine soon afterwards and died there after a short time. In November 1945 my two aunts, my cousin Rena and I were driven out of that area. We reached the North Sea island of Wyck auf Fohr. When my father returned from a French prisoner-of-war camp in 1947 he found me there, the only one of his family left.

In search of work, my father and I ended up on a farm, in a village near Lüchows, about 100 kilometres south-east of Hamburg. At that time the most remarkable thing for me was that boys in the village invited me to a Sunday School! I could not imagine what a Sunday School was, and thought that it involved fairy tales. In that frame of mind I went with the boys to the first session, which was held in the only room belonging to a nun who worked there. Every Sunday morning Sister Erna beamed as she told a Bible story. She prayed, and sang many cheering songs with us, like *"God is love"*, and *"When the Saviour appears as King"*. It was clear to me even at that first session that something was happening that had absolutely nothing to do with fairy tales! I was simultaneously both excited and perplexed by that realisation, and so from then on I went regularly to Sunday School.

The following year my father married again, and I soon moved to join his wife in the next village, while my father was busy with farm work several villages further away. My new mother was devoted to me, although she had to work very hard for the farmers as a resident dressmaker, for a daily wage of just 3 Deutschmarks.... fortunately plus free board! I continued to attend Sunday School regularly as before, regardless of the weather. So through Sister Erna's faithful service, the seed of God's Word, which would one day grow, was planted in my heart.

In 1950, when my father found a job in industry in Westphalia, we moved there. However, in this new place there seemed to be no new faith-kindling fellowship on offer, but rather the opposite. Indeed, because of their criticism of the Bible, the school Religious Education lessons had a destructive effect on me. This was so strong that when I remembered my village Sunday School I always used to think, *"What a shame that these stories in the Bible aren't as true as those I learned from Sister Erna"!* Even an occasional visit to church did not help me in my search for God, as the sermons were largely uncompelling and so could not lead me to a decisive turning point. Yet the glowing wick, my longing for truth, was never extinguished, although many years were to pass before the truths of God really began to become personal to me.

*              *                  *                  *

After finishing my Engineering degree in Hanover, followed by my Ph.D. studies in Aachen, I took up the post of head of the data processing area at the Institute of Physics and Technology in the city of Braunschweig near Hanover in October 1971. My situation at that time could be characterised as follows. *Professionally* I had been very successful. I had passed my degree exams effortlessly, with First Class grades in two subjects. I had gained distinction in my Ph.D., as well as the award of Aachen Technical University's prestigious 'Borchers Plaque' It was not surprising that I had slipped straight into a top job as a scientist! In the meantime, *domestically*, I had married, and with our two children we were a happy family. Indeed, things went well for us in many ways. We had no family, health or financial problems. Many people in a position like that think they do not need to know God or be helped by Him. I am emphasising this because I frequently hear people tell how they have only become open to their need of God's help through a particular personal difficulty. It was not like that for me at all. God's ways with individuals are as varied as there are people on this Earth!

It was not until the autumn of 1972 that a sequence of events ensued which were to satisfy my long-standing desire to know the God of whom Sister Erna had spoken 25 years earlier. In a short space of time two different kinds of mission took place in Braunschweig, both of which I attended regularly with my wife. One was a mission held in the secondary modern school in the area in which we lived, and led by a small Christian group. They used an imaginative method, handing each new visitor a Bible and a red pen. Key statements of the Bible were worked through with the active participation of the listeners, and all the Bible passages we studied were marked with red pen as we went along. At the end of this unusual but effective week of mission we were allowed to keep the Bibles. So my wife and I each had identical Bibles, and when we read them we often came across passages which were already marked, and therefore having for us a certain degree of familiarity.

The other mission took place shortly after the first. It was much bigger: about 2000 people came each day. Here the focus was on quite specific Gospel talks which were definitely designed to lead uncommitted people like us to a decision. The call to faith in God, by deciding to follow His Son, Jesus Christ, went out each evening as a clearly formulated invitation. In the sermon by Leo Janz, based on the Gospel according to Luke, Chapter 17, Verses 33-36, the choice between life *without* God and life *with* Him, was clearly expressed. Indeed, so much so that, after overcoming feelings of reluctance, even *fear* of what might happen next, I followed the general call to go to the front to discuss my personal situation with spiritual counsellors. My wife came too.

Private discussions and prayer with the counsellors were very helpful in bringing us both to personal assurances of salvation. At long last I really began to understand those songs Sister Erna had taught us! I began to feel God's love for me as an individual, and to appreciate that Jesus Christ had died to save me from the consequences of my sins! Remarkably, both the people we talked to belonged to the local Bible study housegroup that we were soon to join. Further days of mission in Braunschweig followed, but our attitudes had changed from ones of *seeking and wanting*, to ones of *learning and satisfaction*. The seeds of truth first sown by Sister Erna were now growing fast!

On some evenings of the days that followed, Pastor Heinrich Kemner spoke in the packed St Martin's Church. Even now his sermon on the prophetic picture of the river flowing from the throne in the temple, described in the Old Testament prophetic book of Ezekiel, Chapter 47, is unforgettable to me. Through that powerful message on the benefits of total commitment to God I was excited to such an extent that I immediately decided to find out where the preacher came from. I had to hear him again! So I was soon on my way to Krelingen, an idyllic heathland village near Walsrode. The days that followed at the Ahlden Youth Mission, under the oaks of Krelingen, left a decisive effect on the growth of my faith in God. Pastor Kemner's books also gave me important boosts and helped me straighten out many of the perspectives I had on life. In particular I learned that when we have found God, He expects us not only to enjoy Him ourselves, but to share knowledge of Him with others, even though our knowledge may, at first, be new, and incomplete. So I learned that God looks to those who have found Him to be His active representatives in the world. I learned, too, that it is not in passing examinations, or developing careers, or even in building stable marriage relationships and happy families, that counts with God - but bearing spiritual fruit for Him, as described in the New Testament Letter of Paul to the Romans,

Chapter 12.

After gaining all these new insights, which led me on to still deeper personal study of the Bible, I came to what was for me a decisive personal realisation: *the Bible in its entirety is the Word of God, and, completely unlike any other literature, bears the absolute seal of truth.* This is the only sure and stable foundation for our lives, proving itself to be completely reliable in all realms of life and thought.

Thus, I not only regained the trust in God's Word which I had known in a childish way at Sunday School, but as a mature adult and well-trained scientist, experienced such confidence in it that I was ready to profess it publicly and pass it on. This I did first through personal testimony now and again in Bible Study sessions which I held in our church. I quickly recognised that belonging to a Bible-believing church, and being brought personally into the life of such a church, are absolutely essential if we want to grow in our everyday commitment to Jesus Christ. In studying the New Testament texts it is clear that those who know God find strength, comfort and inspiration as they seek to worship and serve God together. If someone asks me if it is not equally possible to be a Christian on one's own, I reply thus: *"The probability is just as slim as crossing the Atlantic intact in a canoe. It is almost certain that one will be caught by the waves, and sink miserably!"*

\*                    \*                    \*                    \*

So, what is the nature of my faith in God today? I have come to recognise Jesus as the Christ, the Son of God, the One Who saves me from being lost. His way on this Earth had one prescribed goal: *"The Son of Man came to save what was lost"* (Gospel according to Matthew, Chapter 18, Verse 11). He who came from eternity came from God the Father, became a man, and redeemed us by way of a plan which no merely human intellect could think up. Amid the bawling of the crowd he died in torment on the cross of Golgotha. This was the ransom for my sin, and that of the whole world! Since Jesus was without sin Himself, the power of death had no hold over Him, and so His resurrection from the dead was the seal of victory over all the powers of evil. I am so glad that I was able to hear the call to be His follower, and now belong for ever to that Saviour who is - as the chorus I learnt from Sister Erna asserted - also truly King.

The New Testament also reveals to us that it was through Jesus that God created the whole Universe, as well as this Earth and all the life on it. There are no exceptions, for *"Through Him all things were made; without Him nothing was made that has been made"* (Gospel according to John, Chapter 1, Verse 3). Indeed, it was not only made *through Him*, but also *for Him* as its Lord and King (Paul's Letter to the Colossians, Chapter 1, Verse 16).

This leads me to one of the most elevated of all thoughts: *the Creator and the Man on the cross were one and the same Person*! Whatever moved this Lord of Lords and King of Kings to go to the cross for ME? My understanding cannot fathom this, but in the Gospel according to John, Chapter 3, Verse 16, there is this answer: it was *His boundless love* which did everything for me, so that I might not suffer separation from Him, needlessly, for ever!.

So where am I, and where are you today, in relation to the state of the world, and to this God I first really met in 1972? Humans everywhere are troubled by two kinds of fear - I call them *fear of life*, and *fear of death* We all have the will to live, but each threat fills our life with that fear I call the 'fear of life'. Recently, around 800 secondary school pupils were asked how they felt about the future. Over 700 replied *"Afraid!"* Because of the gigantic build up of arms we see the danger of another world war. All peace marches are basically demonstrations of fear. Pollution and dying forests, shortages of energy, over-population, and increasing crime characterise the world today. It is with good reason that we fear the future.

But added to all these fears of life is also the 'fear of death', and this weighs heaviest of all. Many ask *"What happens after death?.... Where do I spend eternity?"* Through the personal commitment of my life to God, I have experienced a real release from the fears of both life and death! This release can be characterised in three ways: it involves *real peace*, *real love*, and *faith that works*. We cannot generate these things ourselves, only receive them as gifts from God.

REAL PEACE defies all our attempts to understand it, and cannot be generated by any human activity: its source is God, and it is His gift to those who will receive it. The New Testament tells us in the Gospel according to John, Chapter 14, Verse 27, that Jesus said to His temporarily disheartened disciples *"My peace I give you.... Do not let your hearts be troubled, and do not be afraid."* I first began to experience that peace myself after I met God in 1972.

REAL LOVE is just as amazing! We begin to discover its supreme dimensions only when we trust ourselves to God's care. The Apostle Paul, writing to the early church in Rome, said this of the love of God: *"I am convinced that neither death, nor life, neither angels, nor demons, neither the present nor the future, nor any powers, neither height nor depth, nor anything else in creation, will be able to separate us from the love of God that is in Christ Jesus our Lord."* (Paul's Letter to the Romans, Chapter 8, Verses 38-39).

And FAITH THAT WORKS is faith in the good news that through Jesus Christ we can enjoy fellowship with God every day. This faith is not some vague general belief, nor performance of any religious rite, but simple trust in Him. For this life I am glad to be able to entrust myself to the wise Creator of the Universe; and for the life to come I look forward to being with Him, as it were, in His own home for ever.

Very early in my life I sensed that the truth that makes sense of everything is in the Bible. The conviction I have come to much more recently is both liberating and unequivocal: the Bible is not only a suitable, but also the *absolutely essential* interpretative framework for understanding the world, and all life in it. No science can work without suitable premises. I now know, too, that our lives will not work apart from the premises in the Bible, given us by our Creator. If we omit or neglect any part of this divine information, or alter it to fit our own individual opinions, we lose indispensable parts of the mosaic of God's truth. We do this at our peril!

# 4.

# ORDER AND DISORDER

**Professor Kimihisa Murakami**

*(Professor of Civilization and Environment, Seigakuin University, Japan)*

**Professor Murakami** *spent most of his early years in the city of Osaka, on the Japanese island of Honshu. Having gradually become* "aware of the ugliness deep inside" *himself, and his need of God's help to put things right, he became a Christian, and was baptised just three months before graduating from High School and moving to Kyoto for his university undergraduate and graduate studies. Majoring in Forest Science, his chief interests focused increasingly on problems of forest hydrology. Passing an examination for the Japanese Civil Service, he joined the Forestry and Forest Products Research Institute of the Japanese Ministry of Agriculture, Forestry and Fisheries as a research worker. The projects he was engaged on were in the field of tropical forest conservation, related to the Japanese Government's international co-operation programme. In the course of his work he has visited various tropical countries for field work and research in deforestation, especially to plan and manage tree planting activities. He describes the deforestation problem as* "The most critical problem for the global environment from the ecological point of view".
*More recently, along with co-workers in 13 countries, he has established a non-governmental organisation named BIO-REFOR (Biotechnology-assisted Reforestation). This is attempting to preserve*

*tropical forests in the Asia-Pacific region.*

*As a teenage boy, one of his preoccupations was with two fundamental questions:* "How was the Universe put in order originally?" *and* "By whom?" *This chapter, based on the one by Professor Murakami in the Japanese edition* of "Scientists Who Find God", *published by Word of Life Press Ministries in Toyko, Japan, reflects on the answers he found to these questions when a teenager. These are answers which he now shares with students in the Christian University of Seigakuin, in which he lectures.*

---

Japan avoided colonisation by Western great powers, and achieved its own industrialisation at an abnormally fast speed. It was then defeated in World War II. Three years later, Kimihisa Murakami was born in Semba, Osaka, the oldest son of a chemist working for a family dyestuffs business established three centuries earlier. After the War, Japan decided to strengthen its role as a country of trade and commerce. The Japanese people thought Imperial Japan had been defeated by the Allies because they had fallen behind them in science and technology. So, they were eager to imitate the ways of victorious nations. But they were less keen to change their traditional philosophies or to adopt new religions. Thus, there was a generally shallow understanding of Christianity. Kimihisa recalls that when he was a junior high school student, a popular Japanese edition of Bertrand Russell's book *"Why Am I Not a Christian?"* was wrongly entitled *"Are Religions Necessary?"*

Around 300 BC in China, a book of collected poems entitled *"Chushi"* was compiled in the country area of Chu situated around the middle section of the Yangtze River. The book contains nature poems which pose questions concerning the natural world and the Universe. In one such poem, the poet asks Heaven, *"If the light was separated from the darkness, then who did it?"* As a teenage boy, Kimihisa was strongly attracted by similarly fundamental questions, particularly how the present world had been put in order originally, and by whom?

These questions took on greater significance one night when he was 13 years old. Lying in bed he suddenly realised that some day he would die: a dreadful realisation which prevented him from sleeping all night. Several days later, in his father's study, he found a biography of Buddha. This gave him little comfort, for it did not assuage the fear of disappearing eternally from the world, and this fear kept tormenting him.

To make matters worse, the faith of his fathers taught that although there is a god, we cannot get to know him, for he is aloof and distant from mere mortals. As for human beings, that faith teaches that we have many natural desires, each of which is a mixture of good and evil. Somehow we must use them to benefit ourselves and others *through our own self-control*. Kimihisa was sure he did not have enough self-control to achieve much good in the short life which would be his!

Some months later, though, he happened to begin reading a diglot New Testament which his sister had been using for English study. This book had English on the left hand pages, and Japanese on the facing pages. It had been provided by The Gideons International - the organisation which places copies of Bibles or New Testaments in many schools, hotels and hospitals around the world.

At first Kimihisa was attracted most by the beautiful language of the Bible, but soon become increasingly aware that it had much to say about the origins of the Universe, and life in it. Still concerned about dying, he began to ask also *"What is life?"* None of the Biology books he studied at school or as an undergraduate gave a definition of life. One day, though, he came across this sentence: *"Life is a constant struggle against the irreversible tendency of entropy increase."* Entropy is a thermodynamic concept roughly representing the extent of haphazardness in a system. Famous for his studies of the transport of blood around the body, the physician who had written that line regarded life as a ceaseless battle - a battle between the life activities sustaining the order of the matter in the living body, and the forces destroying this order, increasing entropy in tissues of the body, and leading inevitably to its death.

Kimihisa was sent by his parents to a school where the Christian faith was taught - a school which had been founded in the Meiji Era by a Southern Baptist missionary from the USA. This choice of school was based on the good education it provided. Teachers at the school helped him to realise that it was *God* who had created, and brought order, to the Universe.... and it is He Who brings order to each individual living thing also. Kimihisa had wondered *"Who put the Universe in order?"* He found this decisive answer in the first book of the Bible, the Book of Genesis: *"In the beginning GOD created the heavens and the earth."* The Chinese poet had asked *"If the light was separated from the darkness, who did it?"* Again, Genesis gave the answer: *"Now the earth was formless and empty, darkness was over the surface of the deep.... And God said, 'Let there be light', and there was light.... and he separated the light from the darkness"*. But most remarkable of all for Kimihisa was the general message of the Bible, that this God really loves and cares for His creation, especially for human beings!

At school Kimihisa became increasingly aware of ugliness deep within himself, and learnt it was this natural evil which prevented him from being able to know the loving Creator God and enjoy His help personally. Little by little it dawned on him that new order could be brought into his experience because God's Son, Jesus Christ, had suffered and died on the cross at Calvary, once and for all breaking the power of death, and opening the way to everlasting life. Just before graduating from high school he accepted that Jesus Christ had died for him, and asked God to give him new life - *spiritual life* which, though his body would die, he would enjoy for ever. Death was no more to be feared, but was the gateway to heaven! Overcoming the opposition of his family, Kimihisa was baptised - the death of his *old self* being signified as he went down under the water, and the birth of his *new self* being pictured as he emerged again from it.

In the years which have followed that life-changing period, Professor Murakami has thought more about the origins of everything, and suggests that the thermodynamic concept of entropy can be used to summarise and explain the Christian understanding of life, the Universe we live in, and God's role in relation to both. Entropy, remember, is low when things are well ordered, and high when they are confused and disordered.

Professor Kimihisa Murakami invites us to consider the case of the physical Universe as a whole. The world we live in is complex, yet beautifully ordered. We see this order at every level, from the sub-microscopic to the galactic, and in this there is clear, strong evidence of a Creator. The Bible affirms that the physical Universe was created by God; it affirms, too, that He is still *"sustaining all things by his powerful word"* (Letter to the Hebrews, Chapter 1, Verse 3). No wonder then, that the *"heavens declare the glory of God"* (Psalm 19, Verse 1), and that *"the whole earth is full of his glory"* (Isaiah Chapter

6, Verse 3). One day, though, this Universe will disappear. Speaking of that time, the Bible prophesies that *"The heavens will disappear with a roar; the elements will be destroyed by fire, and the earth and everything in it will be laid bare."* (Second Letter of Peter, Chapter 3, Verse 10). What the Bible does *not* tell us is *when* that will happen, saying instead that this day will *"come like a thief"*, (Paul's First Letter to the Thessalonians, Chapter 5, Verse 2), unexpected and unannounced.

Professor Murakami further reflects that just as it was God who brought the Universe into being, and ordered it, so it is God who also brings order into the materials of which men and women are made. As Genesis 2 v. 7 reports, it was God Who breathed into (the first man) Adam, so he became a living soul. So much for the *beginning* of human life; what about its *end*? We have seen that the Bible foretells the end of the world: it also speaks of the ends of our lives on Earth - though once again it does not tell us when these things will be. A human, like any living being faces death when its well-ordered life activities are defeated by forces which destroy that order, resulting in haphazardness and confusion amongst the molecules which had come to be built and function together as its physical body.

Kimihisa contrasts this disorder, and its cause, with the order God designed and originally intended there should be. Mankind was designed to be secure and happy in his recognition of God as his maker, protector and friend. At first that was how it was. In the poetic language of Genesis, God and man are portrayed walking together, companionably, in a garden in the cool of the evening - the best time of the day. But Genesis also tells of the intrusion of sin into this idyllic situation - and of the extreme disorder this initiated. The most immediate result was the separation of human beings from God.... followed by eventual physical death for everyone.... and blood, sweat and tears for us all whilst trying to keep our bodies alive in a now hostile environment - outside the original garden paradise. Worst of all, human sin deadens us to God, leaving our spiritual lives naturally aimless and disordered, haphazard in the extreme.

But there is *hope for everyone*! Kimihisa appreciates that the true glory of the Bible message lies in the wonderful paradox which he first appreciated as a teenager! The paradox that through His death on the cross at Calvary, Jesus Christ broke the power of death itself, and opened the way for new spiritual life and orderliness to be secured for all. The same God Who separated light from darkness can give us this new life because of the death of His Son! True, as a remaining legacy of sin, sooner or later our bodies die, but knowing that everlasting spiritual life is available to everyone who acknowledges God's control of their life, the fear of death no longer torments Kimihisa, and need not torment anyone at all!

Kimihisa concludes: *"I have been observing natural phenomena, and especially life phenomena, for years of my life as a research worker. The longer I have studied, the more I have become convinced that this world did not come into being accidentally, but was created, and is maintained, by God.... I am also sure that I am kept alive by the Creator, and since I have found God I have been able to enjoy the knowledge that I am allowed to live in His love. Bertrand Russell was indeed a great philosopher, but he did not know God, and both he, and those who translated - or MIStranslated - his writings into Japanese therefore COMPLETELY MISUNDERSTOOD the greatest mysteries of the Universe! It is these mysteries, explained in the Bible, that Japanese people, indeed people everywhere, need to explore seriously, and understand before it is too late."*

# 5.

# WHENCE LIFE IN THE UNIVERSE?

### Dr. Michael Leggett
*(Industrial Research Chemist, Turriff, Grampian Region, Scotland)*

*Life is often described as a journey. For many it is also a puzzle. For many more it is a series of problems. For a few - like Dr. Michael Leggett, research chemist living in the small Highlands town of Turriff, Grampian Region, Scotland - it is a PLEASURE, although in his case it only became so relatively recently.*

*Amongst Dr. Leggett's wide-ranging personal interests Chemistry, Pharmacology, Astronomy and Psychology have long figured importantly. He is a Fellow of the Royal Society of Chemistry, the Royal Astronomical Society, and the British Interplanetary Society. He also has an on-going interest in Psychology, as befits a former pupil of a school in Spalding, England which had been founded by a disciple of the world-renowned psychologist, Sigmund Freud.*

*From an early age Michael Leggett was fascinated to know whether the Universe had come about by chance. This most fundamental question concerned him through his school and college days, into his Bachelor of Science degree studies in the University of Nottingham and his Doctor of Philosophy researches in the University of the West of England. Recently, however, that question has been answered, with highly beneficial consequences for Michael.*

*Like many ordinary journeys at one point or another, Dr. Leggett's journey through life has involved a significant change in direction.*

*It was whilst researching for his Ph.D. in Chemistry that the full implications of what Dr. Leggett himself describes as "three pivotal episodes" in his experience dawned upon him, causing him to consciously and deliberately seek radical changes in his life, and the direction in which it was heading. Dr. Leggett describes himself before these changes as "conceited and confused"; after those changes, he has become "humble and convinced".*

*Why humble, and convinced of what? Read on!*

------------

Both my personal outlook on life, and its general direction, have recently undergone a total change. So, too, has my experience of life, which has undergone a dramatic change for the better. Let me tell you how.

I am a very analytical person. This is probably one reason why I have become a professional research chemist. Therefore, I have recently reviewed, and tried to analyze, how and why my life has changed so totally. I would be surprised and disappointed if there were not many other people who could identify with some of the situations I have been in, the questions life itself has posed me, and therefore the conclusions which I have reached.

In particular, I have been fascinated by this question: *"Has life in the Universe arisen spontaneously?"* Or, put differently, *"Is Nature ALONE responsible for life, including the life of mankind - morally and ethically such a sophisticated species?"*

Let me recount three episodes which have illuminated these questions for me, and have proved pivotal, literally turning my life right around. I will describe them in chronological order.

The first such episode was in my teens. At that time I lived in eastern England, near a town called Spalding. I attended the local day secondary school. But I was absolutely miserable there. For me, as for many people, adolescence was a time of crisis. Because of my distress at being bullied by gangs of other boys, my parents took me from that school and sent me to a different one, called Red Hill School. Although I was generally happy at that school, and received a good education from it, I soon became aware of its unusual history, and the influence this still had on what it taught: Red Hill School was founded by one Otto Shaw, a firm believer in Sigmund Freud's views on Psychology.

One of Freud's most widely publicised views is that the Judaeo-Christian belief in God is no more than a neurotic fixation on a convenient, but imaginary, 'father figure'. Contrary to the belief in God as a great Creator being which that faith holds, Freud propounded that mankind had evolved naturally. Religious beliefs of any kind were therefore both unnecessary and undesirable. Freud went even further: he theorized that anyone who had religious beliefs was ill, and needed psychoanalytic therapy!

However, despite its strong links with Freudian psychology, Red Hill School was not totally closed to God. Indeed, the Matron was a devout Christian, and she gave me several books that caused me to question whether Freud had been right about religion or not. One thing which soon occurred to me was that religious belief was at least no more neurotic than atheism: if faith in God as the Creator and Father of all mankind was indeed a 'neurotic father fixation', was not the faith of the atheist akin to the common neurotic fantasy of childhood that we are orphans, only adopted by the adult with whom we live?!

One other thing particularly impressed me at that time, through the books the Matron gave me. One of these had been written by a 'general practitioner', or 'family doctor' as these local health experts are more popularly known in Britain. This doctor drew attention to remarkably advanced community-health instructions which had been issued about 15 centuries before the time of Christ by the Jewish patriarch Moses, thousands of years before the work of Louis Pasteur, or the formulation of the first germ theory. For example, Moses effectively encouraged his compatriots to use quarantining of infected people - and burning of their contaminated garments - to prevent communicable diseases from becoming epidemic. The details are recorded to this day in Chapter 13 of the Biblical book of Leviticus. These health instructions given in Leviticus were later employed with success in Europe, nearly 3000 years afterwards! I found it difficult to understand how such instructions could have emerged from a relatively primitive society unless there really was a God Who, as the Bible claimed, cared about the race of men He had created, and Who was somehow able to communicate with human beings. So I began to grow aware of some strongly conflicting views concerning the origins of man. This was the *first* pivotal experience in my personal growth and development.

*                *                *                *

The *second* pivotal episode did not take place until, during, and immediately after my studies for my first university degree. From 1978-1981 I studied at the University of Nottingham in midland England, and graduated with a good Bachelor of Science degree with Honours in Chemistry and Pharmacology. One type of class we had to attend in Nottingham University was the 'tutorial', a small group discussion class. During one of my Pharmacology tutorials, my tutor, Professor James Crossland, made reference to the famous Biblical account of the conversion of Paul on the road from Jerusalem to Damascus. Paul had been a very active persecutor of the early Christians, and was on his way to attack the church in Damascus. In the Biblical book called *"The Acts of the Apostles"* it is recorded that all of a sudden Paul saw a brilliant light in the sky, and heard a voice asking, *"Paul, why are you persecuting Me?"* Paul was sure it was God speaking to him, rebuking him strongly for his militant campaign against the teaachings of Jesus Christ. As a result, Paul abandoned his persecution of the Christian community and, indeed, went on to become one of the greatest communicators of the Christian gospel in the whole of history.

Professor Crossland's argument was that Paul's Damascus road experience was not a true vision of God, but a mental aberration caused by an epileptic attack! At home in Spalding I recounted this to a friend who, like me, attended the local branch of the prestigious Royal Astronomical Society. I went on to remark that, in my opinion, Professor Crossland had not gone far enough: in my opinion ALL religious experiences could be explained by neuropsychiatric illness, or psychoactive drugs and toxins!

My friend however, politely disagreed! He referred me to a book by the famous author and philosopher, Professor C.S.Lewis of Cambridge University, called *"The Abolition of Man"*. In it, Professor Lewis questions whether any of us have any right or justification to claim a deeper, or different, understanding of the experiences of someone else: could another person really understand an experience better than the person who had actually had it? I was greatly impressed by that argument! It convinced me that it is much too easy to dismiss things we do not understand, including many experiences of others - instead of trying to learn from them.

Returning to the specific case of Paul, I am now sure that his own pivotal experience on the road to Damascus could not have been an epileptic fit, or seizure of any kind. The Biblical account confirms that it was indeed Paul who saw the 'great light from heaven'.... but the Bible also affirms that Paul was not alone in hearing the voice of God: those travelling with him heard it also! The book of The Acts of the Apostles, Chapter 9, Verse 7 says his companions did not see anyone else as Paul fell to the ground - but they certainly heard the voice of someone speaking to him!

*                    *                    *                    *

The *third* episode that has helped to radically change my life was even more recent. After I had graduated from the University of Nottingham with my Bachelor of Science degree, I began to research in the University of the West of England for my Doctor of Philosophy degree in Chemistry. At the same time my interests in Astronomy continued to intensify. By 1983 I had learnt enough to be able to give a series of talks to the Bristol Branch of the Royal Astronomical Society on the theme of *"Life in the Universe"*. These talks dealt with the astronomical requirements for a planet to support life forms of the kinds familiar to us on Earth.... and with the current search for intelligent life on other planets.

In order to give these talks, I had to think very carefully about the questions they raised. In particular, I began to think more deeply about the origin and evolution of life on Earth than I had ever done before. As I did so, I became more and more dissatisfied with the increasingly fashionable concepts which seek desperately to find purely biological justifications for things which distinguish mankind from the rest of the animal kingdom, including ethics and morality. And I became very impressed by the recollection from one of the books lent to me by my school Matron that the 'Ten Commandments', as we call them, that basic set of laws for living reported by the Bible to have been given by God to Moses, were so far ahead of their time that they could only have originated from Someone who had a deep understanding of both mankind's physical and spiritual needs.

I recalled, too, another point by Professor Lewis. In that book of his, *"The Abolition of Man"*, Professor Lewis wrote of two tourists who visited a waterfall. One tourist called the waterfall 'pretty'; the second called it 'sublime'.

Professor Lewis ridiculed an anonymous author he had recently read. That author had implied that, when someone suggests that an object is 'sublime'.... or 'praise-worthy'.... or 'contemptible'...., that person is making a subjective emotional judgement which has no basis in reality. Lewis contended that it would be only a 'trousered ape' - an ape dressed like a man but incapable of thinking like one - who would conceive of some physical feature as the Atlantic as nothing more than many million tons of cold salt water. Meanwhile, part of being human is the ability to discern that some things are aesthetically or ethically superior, whilst others are grossly inferior, for C.S.Lewis argued that objects *"not merely receive, but.... merit, our approval or disapproval, our reverence, or our contempt"!*

Later in the same book Lewis concluded that *"The man who called the waterfall sublime was not intending simply to describe his own emotions about it: he was also claiming that the object was one which merited those emotions. This is the doctrine of 'objective value' - the doctrine that certain attitudes are really true.... to the kind of thing the Universe is and (true to) the kind of things we are."* To help us understand this important concept, Lewis explained that some objects and actions RESONATE with the reality of the Universe and of our human nature, whilst other objects are DISSONANT to, and destructive of, the Universe as it really is.

After reading Lewis, I knew it was absurd to believe that rational thoughts could have grown up spontaneously through the working of irrational natural forces. It made little enough sense to believe nature had made itself; it was *absolutely ludicrous* to believe nature had EDUCATED itself to recognize values that resonated with reality! I came to see only one logical explanation for all of this: at the very beginning of the Universe there must have been a highly rational Being. He it was who created mankind, and deliberately made us different from other life on Earth! So I realised that this great Being, God as we call Him, is the essential reference point, in whose light not only the Bible makes sense, but humanity too.

\*                    \*                    \*                    \*

It was these three episodes together that caused me to see that natural processes alone are totally inadequate to explain the origins of intelligent life of Earth, and the religious experiences that so many people, both past and present, have clearly had. This was the intellectual framework which forced me to acknowledge that there must be a God at work in the Universe: and, if so, that He could work in my own life also.

So I began to attend a local church, hoping that, through this channel, I would discover enough about God to find Him myself. Certainly most people there already knew Him. They were warm and friendly, and clearly enjoyed worship and Bible study. Within a few days I responded to an invitation to speak to God myself, to seek His forgiveness for my past wrongdoings, and to receive power to live the way my conscience knew I ought to live.

Since then I have come to appreciate that the Christian life is less of a destination than a journey. There is still much I do not know or understand about God's purposes and ways of working. But I do know that, *spiritually*, I feel at peace at last; *intellectually*, I am confused no longer; and *practically*, as a member of human society, I am becoming a much better person. I used to be conceited and arrogant, and proud of my own achievements. In my personal relationships with others I was very selfish, seeking only to take, but never to give. I used to drink alcohol heavily, which was undermining my whole life. Now, since becoming a Christian I realise that I cannot achieve anything without abilities given me by God. I am finding I want to seek out ways of helping others. And soon after meeting God for the first time I reached the point at which I actually wanted to give up alcohol completely.

I am aware of the impossibility that the Universe in general, and mankind in particular, could have come about by chance. For it was this realisation that caused me to search for the Creator and Sustainer of everything: His life pre-dated the Universe, brought it to birth, and pervades it through and through. Trying to live without His help is therefore a most illogical, and in practice, much lower form of existence than He means life to be. Thus, it was through finding God for myself that my life has become a *pleasure* rather that a series of never-ending problems. And it is by God's help that my life is now becoming so much more worthwhile.

# 6.

# FREEDOM FROM THE 'SELFISH OPPRESSORS'

### Dr. Tom Hartman
*(Postdoctoral Research Fellow in Life Sciences, University of Nottingham, England)*

*Someone whose name is Thomas Peter Vitezslav Hartman is likely to have a mixed, and interesting, family background! This is certainly true of* **Dr. Tom Hartman**, *for although he was born in England, he has several different Central European elements within even his most immediate family circle.*

*In 1982 Tom left his childhood family home in Wembley Park, Middlesex, England, to read for an Honours Degree in Zoology at the University of Bristol. It was here the Editor met Tom, just after his graduation, and was greatly impressed by the unusually mature grasp this young man had not only of the Science of Zoology, but perhaps more unexpectedly, of its philosophy.*

*Tom went on from Bristol to research successfully for his Ph.D. degree in the University of Manchester, England, sponsored by SERC (the British Science and Engineering Research Council). His research topic was "Pest Management by Cytogenetics", a technique whereby the reproduction of unwanted species is deliberately disrupted by human manipulation of its chromosomes. This topic suited Tom very well, because he had long been fascinated by Genetics, and by the attendant arguments in Sociobiology concerning the extent of the power of genes in shaping animal behaviour. For many years he wondered whether genes might really be, as some popular scientists have suggested, 'selfish oppressors', from whose grip humans alone can be free.... ?*

*In this Chapter, updated from a radio script prepared with Dr. Barrett just before Dr. Hartman left the University of Bristol, Tom leads us along the path he has followed from first recognising the problem of the 'selfish oppressors', to debating and experimenting with possible solutions to this question, and finally to finding personal peace and satisfaction through the very practical answer he has found.*

---

Some things in my life have been very complicated, but others have been, and are, much more simple. My family background is a good example of things far from simple.

I was born in England, and my family home is at Wembley Park, not far from the world-famous sports arena, Wembley Stadium. However, ethnically I am half Czech and half Swiss, for my father is from the Czech Republic, and my mother from Switzerland. I have three sisters, two of whom are half-sisters, born to my father's first wife, who died in the early 1950s. Since she was Russian, these two of my sisters are half Czech and half Russian! In 1988 I married Jenny, a woman I met while at Bristol University. Oddly enough, I have even strengthened my links with central Europe through her, as she is a descendant of a Russian family who lived in Odessa in The Ukraine. She is the last of the Sakoshansky family, whose surname does not occur anywhere else in the UK!

My interest in Science, though, is a good example of things much more simple. As far back as I can remember I have always been interested in the biological sciences. In one way it seems as if I never had any choice in this.

As soon as I became aware of other living things I was fascinated with Biology. This must have begun as early as the age of four or five! And I think I soon became much more serious about studying it than many other kids of my age. One reason for this was that I am asthmatic. When I was young there were not the same drugs to control the disease that we have now. Today asthma still causes me discomfort and even some pain.... but does not put me in hospital any more. But when I was a child it often troubled me seriously, and I spent a lot of time in bed. So I read widely. And when I got better, and was able to go out again, I began collecting biological specimens, such as insects in the park. Then I got interested in reptiles.... especially dinosaurs.... and still am! When still quite young I dug two ponds in our back garden to rear newts, though this pales a bit in comparison with an expedition I was involved in during 1995 to trap Nile crocodiles in Zululand! We took measurements from them and then released them as part of an ongoing ecological research project, looking at the role of crocodiles in the lakeland ecosystem.

My days as a 'young naturalist' came to an enforced end in my early teens: I was sent to boarding school! Although I was not a boarder myself, I still had to suffer the long school day, from 8.45 in the morning until 6.15 in the evening. There just was no time left to go on indulging my interests out of doors. So I turned to the more academic aspects of the biological sciences instead. I spent a lot of time in the laboratory, and looking at life through the microscope, I found this even more fascinating than outdoor observation. I taught myself a lot of Biology, and learnt more through my school lessons, so I had little difficulty preparing for the university qualifying exams. Three years later I duly graduated from the University of Bristol with a good Honours Degree in Zoology. From 1985 to 1989, under the sponsorship of a Research Studentship, I worked towards a Ph.D. degree at the University of Manchester. This research award was from 'SERC', the British Science and Engineering Research Council. The topic was the management of insect pests by cytogenetic means. Maybe I should explain a little.

The control of pests by manipulation of their chromosomes is a well established practice. For example, major insect pests such as the screwworm (which affects cattle), and the Mediterranean fruit fly, are regularly suppressed by releasing into the environment billions of males that have been made completely sterile by disturbing their chromosomes. These males mate with wild females who will produce no offspring. My own research focused on a more refined use of this technology. Instead of completely disrupting the entire chromosome complement of the animals, I tried to breed flies that were only partially disturbed in this way, through only a small number of chromosome rearrangements. This meant that, instead of being completely sterile, the released flies would leave a small number of descendants which would remain in the population, ensuring that it would not die out completely, but the overall population would remain small! This would be much better for the ecosystem generally as there would always be flies to service the needs of predators - birds and spiders - so these would not suffer too. This strategy should also ensure that no gap in the ecosystem would be created for flies from other areas to invade, perhaps once more leading to the problems large populations of them can cause.

From Manchester, I then moved to Birmingham where I worked on more academic aspects of chromosome biology and spent some time in one of the hospitals looking at the chromosome mutations suffered by African uranium miners. I then spent a period working as a Park Ranger, helping to care for an area of woodland and taking school children and interested members of the public on natural history walks - the enthusiasm shown by some of the kids to learn about other living things reminding me of my own eagerness when I was young!

At the moment, I am based at the University of Nottingham, where I am using my experience of chromosome biology to work on a project funded by the UK Overseas Development Agency. This work is concerned with the stability of rice plants that have been hybridised with wild species to give them better yields and make them more tolerant of poor conditions. The techniques that I am using are some of the most dramatic available, enabling me to pinpoint clusters of genes to their precise physical locations on the chromosomes. We are hoping to study the chromosomes of the hybrids, where the parents have very different characteristics, and observe how the two sets of parental genes interact. These hybrids carry a lot of hopes with them as they are being produced in an effort to stave off world hunger in the 21st century, when human populations seem certain to be much higher than they are even today.

I am sure that these researches have wider implications too, involving moral considerations, and even the fundamental philosophies of life itself. For example, since the mid-1970s it has been generally accepted that one of the biggest revolutions in Biology has been the rise of 'sociobiological' theories.... theories insisting that the role of an individual animal is to survive merely to reproduce, and so propagate its genes into the next generation. However, if my present research with rice plants succeeds, then we will have a new example of human activity significantly changing the natural world. In this case, mechanisms that have kept plant species separate for millennia can be overcome speedily in the laboratory. In the case of the research with flies, cytogenetics causes individual life and reproduction to promote not the continuation, but actually the *decline* of the species.

But my own interest in the theories and implications of Sociobiology certainly do not end there. Many animals are clearly programmed by their genetic material to behave in the general ways they do. So, a fascinating question is this: *"To what extent may it be said that we, as members of the human species, are programmed by our genes also?"*

This question involves some of the key tenets of Sociobiology. In 1976 a book on Sociobiology was published which was to become very influential in this field. It is called *"The Selfish Gene"*. Written by an English biologist, Professor Richard Dawkins, it postulates that people are different from other animals in one very significant respect: we are the only animals who can understand the principles of life and death and reproduction. All other animals are programmed to be selfish: they are selfish so they can reproduce and thus pass on their genetic formulae to their offspring. But we, alone in the Animal Kingdom, are able to *rebel* against the power of those 'selfish genes'!

The implications of this postulate are profound indeed. If it is true, then in the Animal and Plant Kingdoms, *people alone* have the ability to live UNselfishly.... *we alone* can be altruistic, putting the needs of others of our kind above our own, consciously doing our best to help others, even outside our own intimate family circles!

Now if that sounds as if we should be able to improve the quality of life in our society through our own conscious, individual efforts, it has to be admitted that we do not see too much evidence of this in the modern world, with all its problems! Indeed, my own experience strongly suggests that even if we consciously try to live altruistically - and admittedly there are many people who obviously do not even try! - many, if not all, our efforts end in dismal failure.

I must confess that, when I first came across that book by Professor Dawkins, it appealed to me very greatly. For years I had been interested in human, as well as animal, behaviour. And I had often wondered this: could there be anything worth us living for? Perhaps, I thought, I could find out by observing the lives of my friends. So I started keeping notebooks on what they did! And it was written in code, in case any of my friends ever came across them, and disapproved of the nature and details of their contents....

....for I was *not* impressed by what I saw! To be truthful, much of what my friends did was rather nasty! Indeed, most other people seemed to me to be extremely selfish! However, Dawkins seemed to offer hope. Remember, he suggested that people were different from animals: we alone have the ability to rebel against those genes which make animals so selfish.

*"If this is the case"* I said to myself, *"I WILL REBEL! I will be really different from other animals! I will go to great lengths to help other people.... I will be truly altruistic towards my fellow men and women! I will listen to them, really help them. If I do not have to be selfish, then I WON'T!"*

Sadly, as time passed, I grew more and more disillusioned, first with that suggestion, but much more with myself. You see, I had to admit that no amount of personal effort was turning me into the kind of person I wanted to be. My attempts to be unselfish largely ended in failure! I wanted to help others, but my own wishes and desires constantly got in the way. Perhaps the only crumb of comfort I could find was that my experience seemed to match the experience of many other folk who had tried, as I had done, to put other people first! Then, after agonising much, I began to realise that there might be just *one way* through which both others and myself could live lives of true goodness and quality.

So, let me recount the very last time I agonized over my failure to make myself a better person! I was alone in my room one night. *"Can no-one be free from the selfish oppressors - the genes?"* I pled within myself.

Then, very suddenly, like a neon light inside my mind I saw - or thought - or heard - an answer to my question, two words, that were to change my entire outlook on life, change the whole way I was to live. What were those words? *"JESUS WAS!"*.... JESUS was free from the 'selfish genes'! And how was this realisation to change my life? By making me realise it was possible to be free from the 'selfish oppressors', of course!

Where those two words came from into my mind at that particular point in time, I did not know. My family never discussed religion. We were neither positively nor negatively disposed towards it. We had no attitude towards it at all. It was as if religion did not exist! I had never read the Bible for myself. And I had never been able to pray to God. But that night, in my room, everything suddenly changed! I sat back revelling in the sudden, entirely unexpected, yet marvellous revelation: that Jesus Christ had been different from everybody else who had ever lived. The effect on me was literally like the calming of a storm.

From that night on I began to read and study the Bible, to discover more about the life and ministry of Jesus Christ, for the Bible is the major source book on His life and teachings. As I did so I began to understand something of His uniqueness as the One Who, in some mysterious way, was God in a human body: the reason why Jesus was able to live the only perfect life anyone has ever lived. His life on Earth was totally unselfish, as both the Bible and contemporary historians assert. The Bible says that He was *"tempted in every way, just as we are, yet was without sin"* (Letter to the Hebrews, Chapter 4, Verse 15). The Bible also records His teaching that we should therefore *"Love the Lord your God with all your heart"* and *"your neighbour as* [you love] *yourself."* (Gospel according to Matthew Chapter 22, Verses 37 and 39). The Bible amply confirms that Jesus, alone amongst the men of His day did this, but that God now makes such actions conceivable for ordinary men and women if they trust and obey Him.

It is sometimes said that the primary reason why Jesus Christ lived was so that He might pass on His life to others. But the life He came to pass on to us was not *physical* life, as with us and all other animals: it was *spiritual* life. To make this gift possible, He had to sacrifice Himself, to atone for all our sins before God. Only in this way would God be prepared to cause our minds and souls to be reborn, recreated in the image of His own. And, perhaps most remarkably of all, Jesus did not die just for friends and relatives: He died so that *everyone* could live - His many enemies included!

As I write, I have to say that since becoming a Christian I have been through many different situations, some of which still mystify me, and there is a lot about God I still do not understand. But the Lord has been faithful and merciful to me, and my life is really different from what it used to be. I find I am now much more ready to truly put other people first. And I have come to appreciate the company of Christians very much! They did not used to impress me at all. I used to think them whimpish. But early in my Christian life I began to see that many Christians are tough, mentally as well as physically: they can stand up to ridicule and criticism! Also, I used to be something of a loner. But then I began to enjoy the company of other people, especially in church. You remember I never used to read the Bible. But now it goes everywhere with me - to the Lofoten Islands off northern Norway, to the Pyrenees between France and Spain, more recently on that crocodile hunt to Zululand. Wherever I am I read it, because it is God's Word, and it helps and teaches me so much. So, since that memorable evening in my room, I have felt myself being drawn closer and closer to God. It is as if I am getting to know Him personally, and it is good to speak to Him in prayer.

Last but not least, I would like to comment on where some new experiences and new understandings like mine leave Sociobiology as it applies to the human species. The most important question seems to be this: *"Is there any validity at all for the human experience in the concept of the 'selfish gene'?"*

I think there is, although I am sure much ordinary human behaviour is strongly self-centred. People instinctively protect themselves, and put their own interests first, as the Bible often says they do. Sociobiology gives us an explanation for this behaviour from the standpoints of Biology. But I cannot accept that Sociobiology satisfactorily explains all human behaviour: it certainly does not explain life as God intended it should be lived by you or me. Indeed, there is a *fundamental weakness* in the sociobiological arguments, for they totally fail to accommodate the uniqueness of the life of Jesus Christ, and His totally unselfish sacrifice for us all on the Cross of Calvary!

I must conclude. The Bible is not a scientific text, nor was it ever intended to be one. However, I find the Bible to be very accurate, both in its portrayals of human nature, and its analyses of human psychology. Also, its message is accessible to people at all levels of education. Therefore, although the Bible is an ancient book, it is clearly fresher, and more relevant to everyday life, than any scientific hypotheses of Sociobiology.

I began by contrasting some of the *complicated* things in my life with some of the *simple*. It is ironic that, in matters relating to human life and the organisation of human society, many theorists advance highly complex hypotheses - when a few simple, proven, facts clearly set out in the Bible have revolutionized the lives of many people down through the ages, and could still revolutionize the whole world today! Let me leave you with three such facts to marvel at, then act upon:

- *One life* has set the perfect pattern for us all.
- *One death* has covered the spiritual needs of everyone.
- *Through one person*, Jesus Christ, all of us can live truly better lives in the present world, with the added bonus that, if we follow Him in this life, He will then enable us to live with Him throughout eternity.

The 'bottom line' is this: of all life forms on Earth, humans alone can be truly and completely *"free from the selfish oppressors"* - but only with the help of our Creator, God Himself!

# 7.

# PERSONAL EXPERIMENTS

### Dr. David Chadwick
*(Software House Manager, University of Salford, England)*

**Dr. David Chadwick** *is an English graduate with B.Sc. and Ph.D. degrees in Chemistry. Today, he is a Senior Lecturer and researcher in the Information Technology Institute of the University of Salford, a major city in the north west of England. Prior to this he held several responsible positions in the computer industry, including the post of Deputy Director of the Computer Systems Research and Development Section of the University of Salford, and General Manager of Salford Software Services, a division within Salford University Business Services. He is also an author and editor of an International Standard in computer communications.*

*When younger, David had at least partially satisfied a not uncommon urge to travel, by working on a British international aid programme called "Voluntary Service Overseas". This took him to the Republic of Ghana in West Africa as a school teacher of Chemistry. It was whilst in Ghana, on a 'high' from the local crop of marijuana, that he had one of the most frightening experiences of his life: he thought that he was about to die.*

*You see, scientists as a group are trained to experiment. Not many, though, deliberately choose to experiment upon themselves! Dr. Chadwick had been an exception to this since his postgraduate student days, when he began to explore the way his own brain responded to a range of different chemical substances. In this interview David recalls how his experimentation led on to hallucinatory drug addiction.... and being convicted as a drug grower.... but also how personal experimentation of a completely different kind was to save his life, and then, in his own words, to "turn his whole life round!"*

*So, although, by his own admission, David had broken nine of God's 'Ten Commandments', not only was his life spared, but great and unexpected benefits were to accrue from this new, different, overwhelmingly successful, and even miraculous experiment. David explained all this in conversation with Dr. Barrett, when they met after the wedding in Bristol of his brother, Andrew Chadwick, whose own story is outlined in Chapter 11 of this book.*

---

Editor:   Dr. Chadwick, you have an impressive title - *"Postgraduate Course Director, Information Technology, University of Salford"*. Tell us about your job, and what it entails.

David:   I will do my best!

Five years ago I was given the responsibility of starting up a new Master's degree in Managing Information Technology - 'IT' for short. Perhaps I should explain that IT is a comprehensive term covering computer equipment both in hardware and software, and also the business procedures that are used to process, store, manipulate and use information in today's highly complex and automated society. Because of my background, having already been the general manager of a software house, I was ideally placed to know what managers of Information Technology need by way of education, training, and knowledge of the latest developments in this fast-growing field, and how to successfully harness IT for competitive advantage. The Master's course attracts IT professionals from all over the UK and elsewhere, and they study at the University on a part-time basis, taking three or four years to complete their studies. The course is very successful; we even have a managing director from Nigeria commuting to Salford to study on it!

Editor:   This is clearly strategic, as well as challenging, work! But one thing puzzles me: you hold an important position in an IT Institute, but you did not train originally as a computer scientist!

David:    No, I did not. But I had to do a lot of computing for my doctoral research, and I seemed to have an affinity for computers. Computer programming was, for me, the easiest part of my project! Finding I was really interested in computer programming, I gradually moved more and more into this field after finishing my Ph.D.

Editor:   You say you had to do a lot of computing for your Ph.D. What was the title of your research project?

David:    The *"Thermal Decomposition of Methyl Halides"*.

Editor:   Yes.... I feared it would be a topic few of us could understand! And I suspect that asking you for further details might just bemuse most of us even more! But just a sentence or two of simple explanation might be illuminating!

David:    In the laboratory it is possible to heat gases very quickly to about 2000 degrees Celsius using a pulse of energy that moves through the air faster than the speed of sound. Supersonic aircraft such as Concorde create shock waves when they break the sound barrier. Attacked by such shock waves, many gases decompose, at almost the same rates as one another. However, using an instrument called a 'Time-of-flight Mass Spectrometer', the decomposition products can be identified, as well as the sequence in which they are generated. The results can then be compared with computer models, and predictions made for the decomposition sequences of the various substances.

Editor:   That is still very technical, David! Perhaps most of us would more easily appreciate the practical applications to which the results can be put?

David:    I am ashamed to say I never considered what the applications might be! But to be quite truthful, this is largely because I was not really interested in my research. I did it because it seemed less hard work than getting a job!
          And it was during that time that I became aware of *other* chemicals which came to interest - and affect me - a whole lot more!

Editor:   As a supervisor of many Ph.D. students over the last few
          years I confess I am somewhat shocked when you say you
          studied for a Ph.D., but were *"not really interested"* in your
          research!  But perhaps I shall be even more shocked by the
          *other* things you have to confess!  For example, when you
          speak of 'other chemicals'.... do you mean you came to
          experiment with - hallucinogenic drugs?

David:    Yes, I am afraid I do!  I made friends with some guys in my
          Hall of Residence who used hallucinogenic drugs frequently -
          LSD, cannabis, opium, amphetamines, mushrooms.... And it
          was not long before I decided to try some too.  I began with
          cannabis.  At first when I did so, I felt great.  But, although
          some folk say cannabis is not addictive, I can assure you it is!
          Soon I was taking it every day, especially when I had
          repetitive things to do.  Things like series of tests in the
          laboratory, or just driving around.  Cannabis heightens
          physical sensitivity.  It makes life seem funny.  Common
          things may even seem hilarious!  So I would get high on
          cannabis to make life more exciting.
          Then, sometimes, I began to take LSD instead.  This induces
          fantasies, full of colour.  Just a ten thousandth of a gramme
          sends you on a 12-hour trip into unreality!

Editor:   You *almost* make the effects sound desirable!  But, as you
          say, these drugs are addictive, and have other serious and
          frightening effects as well.  Tell us something about these.

David:    After taking cannabis regularly for three or four years, I found
          I could not sleep unless I was strongly under the influence of
          this drug.  Without realising it, I became more and more
          addicted to cannabis, and I would spend hours, days, trying to
          obtain more.
          Meanwhile, the dangers of LSD were more immediately
          obvious.... My LSD 'trips' were unpredictable.  They might be
          good or bad.... and one never knew in advance which they
          would turn out to be!  Often after taking LSD it would be like
          living a nightmare, surrounded by weird beasts and other
          frightening images.
          But worst of all, as a chemist I knew that with all the drugs I
          was taking there was always the risk that they contained
          poisonous contaminants which might very quickly cause

damage, even permanent damage, to my mind or body.

Editor: That was surely a grim time of your life. Did things get better then, or worse?

David: It depends on how you look at it. On the *credit* side, I somehow managed to complete successfully my Doctor of Philosophy thesis. Also, I came to recognise and acknowledge that I was now a drug addict.

But, on the *debit* side I had begun growing cannabis in the University Hall of Residence where I lived, both for my own needs and those of others. This is illegal in the UK. The Police Drug Squad found out about it, and I was tried, and convicted, as a drug grower. So I had not only become a moral and social deviant: I had acquired a criminal record too!

Worst of all, though, was the damage to my own self-esteem. I had always reckoned myself a very self-reliant person, in complete control of my own life: so it came as a great shock when I realised that I really was not in control of myself at all....! Perhaps, though, that was the very beginning of my rehabilitation - which was to take a long time, as you will discover. Although I could not know this at the time, I had many troubles still ahead of me. But more important than any discovery I made in my scientific research was the discovery that I had a deep personal longing that somehow had to be sorted out.

Editor: And it was this problem which you then set about trying to resolve?

David: In one way, yes. But, at first, I mistakenly tried to repay the more obvious of my debts to society without dealing first with the underlying causes of them in my own life! Looking back, I now realise how crazy that was - and how much more I, and others, had to suffer because of my mistaken belief that, if I tried to do good for others, this would somehow make me a good person, inside as well as out.

Now, there is a programme in the United Kingdom through which young people with special professional or technical skills can elect to work in Developing Countries for a few months or years in return only for their food and lodging. I had a Ph.D. in Chemistry, and had done some evening school teaching. So I applied to become involved in this voluntary programme. I was accepted, and sent to the country of Ghana in West Africa as a Chemistry teacher, in a school for teenagers, on the edge of the rain forest.

Editor: And you could no longer take drugs, because they were not available?

David: Just wait - you are running ahead of me! And, unfortunately, your supposition is wrong!

You see, drugs - marijuana in particular - and alcohol, were there in West Africa too: in fact even more plentifully than in England! Worse still for me, the marijuana was cheaper and stronger than I had known in England.

Sanitary and health conditions were primitive in the region of Ghana where I worked, and as a result of this I caught malaria and other tropical diseases. To be quite honest, I was really ill several times. But this did not stop me smoking marijuana. During one visit to another volunteer worker, I had been reading a book by Carlos Castanada, which describes trips on mescale, an hallucinogen which occurs naturally in the Peyote cactus. In Castanada's book a fly has the power of life and death over people. I got high on some really potent marijuana at the time and, all of a sudden it seemed as if the very same fly was approaching me. The fly was prepared to kill me if I did not acknowledge it as all powerful. I was almost literally scared to death! My whole body shook, and my heartbeat was racing. It seemed that the Devil himself was trying to destroy me! There was nothing I could do in that situation to help myself.

Suddenly, although I had ignored God previously - indeed had never accepted before that there is a God who is good, and able to overcome evil - I found myself praying to this Person I did not know, crying out to Him to save and help me! From that moment on my fear began to subside: *my first experiment with God had been a much needed success*!

Editor: You are saying that, suffering from recurrent malaria, plus the effects of drug addiction, you actually reached a point at which you feared for your life? And in sheer desperation, you cried out to God to help you.... even though you had previously not even accepted that He is real?

David:    Yes, exactly so!  And as I began to recover from that situation, I knew it was God who had helped me! You know, scientists sometimes make great discoveries, through experiments that yield unexpected results. And once they have made a great new discovery, they are keen to map out just how big the discovery is! So it was with me. I had discovered God was real, and that He answered prayer. Subsequently I listened, and heard Him speaking to me in my soul, telling me I should not get high on drugs again.

However, looking back, and in the light of that first successful experiment of mine with God, I can only say that I subsequently behaved very *unscientifically* for some years afterwards: often I disobeyed Him, for, astonishingly, I still preferred to believe I could mostly organise my own life quite adequately, without His help! Sure, I prayed to God whenever I was in trouble, but not when things seemed OK! So at first I did not try to explore fully and precisely who God is, and all the ways in which He might choose to help me.

Before I went to Ghana, I met a girl I loved. After I returned to England we set up house together. Then Sue, my girlfriend, became pregnant - and asked me to marry her! I did, but could still find no real peace or happiness in life. Indeed, in some ways things became worse again. Our baby woke us a lot at night I suffered a lot from drug and alcohol hangovers. Sue and I began to argue. Our marriage seemed to be like a ship on the rocks, ready to sink before it had been going long!

Then, one night, high again on cannabis, and for no reason I could understand at the time, I found a Bible I had had at school as a boy, and opened it - seemingly by chance - at the 'Ten Commandments'. This is the list of rules for life which God gave to the human race through the early Jewish leader Moses, thousands of years ago.

Slowly I read these Ten Commandments, in the third chapter of the Biblical book of Exodus. Let me summarise them, and my shocked reactions to them!

ONE:    *"You shall have no other gods before me."*
        Well, I had disobeyed this because marijuana had been for me a 'green goddess'.

TWO:      *"You shall not make yourself an idol, or bow down to idols, or worship them."*

I certainly worshipped marijuana for many years.

THREE:  *"You shall not misuse the name of the Lord your God."*

I used to swear and blaspheme quite frequently.

FOUR:    *"Remember the Sabbath Day to keep it holy."*

Sunday for me was just like any other day.

FIVE;     *"Honour your father and your mother."*

I had had quite bad arguments with my parents in my teenage years, and disobeyed them.

SIX:        *"You shall not murder."*

Well, at last here was one commandment that I had not broken: but things got worse again as I read on!

SEVEN: *"You shall not commit adultery."*

I had slept with many women in my life.

EIGHT:  *"You shall not steal."*

I had stolen many things (even though some of them had been so small that most people would not consider taking them as stealing.)

NINE:     *"You shall not give false testimony."*

I could not honestly say that I had never told a lie.

TEN:       *"You shall not covet."*

I had thought it was quite natural to want things like a bigger house, or bigger car like the neighbours had.

*Deeply shocked* I reflected on that immediate realisation that, of the ten, the only one I had not broken was number six: I had not killed anyone! For I had broken *all the other nine*! I showed the Ten Commandments to Sue and we read them in bed together. Her life story had not been very different from my own. And her reaction was as shocked as mine.

There and then we realised just how dreadful our lives had been, and how nothing we had tried to do to make our lives better had had any significant or lasting success.

Editor:   Having realised that, what did you do next?

David:   There and then we decided we had to go to church next Sunday, to see if this would help us in some way. We picked a church almost at random - and were most surprised to find how warmly we were welcomed! The sermon was astonishingly relevant to our situation, too. It was from Genesis, the first book in the Bible. The preacher spoke of people eating of what Genesis describes as *"The tree of the knowledge of good and evil"*. I asked myself: *"Could it have been proscribed - forbidden - because it was an hallucinogenic fruit?"* There did not seem to be a direct answer to this question, but our interest had been aroused by this possibility, and we soon learned that the Bible has much to say about problems like our own. So we began to attend church regularly.

It took another couple of years of regular church attendance, though, before Sue and I, amazingly in the same service as each other, came to the point when we finally admitted to ourselves and God that only He could free us from our selfish ways, and make our lives truly happy and successful. On that day, the sermon was about miracles. Comparing notes with Sue afterwards confirmed that we both realised that, without a miracle - a supernatural event - our lives would never really change for the better, for we ourselves had no power to make them truly good. But, I am glad to report, we realised, too, that God had, and has, the power to make this miracle happen! To experience that power in our own lives we had to ask the God who had made us if He would forgive us our past sins, as only He can do, and then give us new natures, new desires, even new power from Himself so we could do the things He wished. We realised that *He alone* was able to give us the wholly new lives we had wanted for so long!

At this point in the service, Sue and I both began to weep. And the tears which washed our faces seemed to be an outward symbol of God washing our souls clean. Unquestionably we became changed people thereafter. We marvelled at the changes we saw in each other. And God has kept changing us since then, making us less moody, more loving - and totally able to live *without even the desire* for drugs or alcohol!

Looking back, I can remember a much earlier opportunity I had had to commit my life to God, when I was only 12 years old. But I was so strong-willed then that I had resisted Him:

more than 20 years of unwholesome experiences were the most immediate result. It was not until I came to the point of admitting I was *totally incapable* of making - unaided - a success of my life, that God could work the miracle in me which I so badly needed. And not surprisingly, all my *real* successes in life came after this point!

In summary, it was in Ghana I first realised God was the only one who could truly help me, but at that time I was so full of scientific scepticism that part of me still did not wish to acknowledge that He is real. But gradually thereafter, I became more and more aware that God *is* real.... as real as the evil spirit in the world, the one the Bible calls 'Satan' or the 'Devil'. I am sorry now that I spent so long serving him, not God. But I am overjoyed that, finally, I let God prove how much He could help me. He has turned my whole life around.... so I am glad I have been able to share my story with you today.

# 8.

# MYSTERIES AND MIRACLES IN CENTRAL SIBERIA

**Alexander Yusov**
*(Former Lecturer in Atheism, Soviet Army, Novosibirsk, Siberia)*

*Coming to personal faith in the God of the Bible was not easy for*
**Alexander Yusov.** *A native of the central Siberian metropolis of*
*Novosibirsk, Alex grew up being taught that there was no God, and*
*never even seeing a Bible until 31 years old. By nature a very*
*pragmatic person, Alexander is most comfortable with facts and*
*figures. In his early twenties he became an engineering graduate of*
*the Building Construction Institute in the Siberian city of Novosibirsk.*
*Joining the army of the former USSR as a civil engineer, and*
*convinced that the basic tenets of scientific atheism were not just*
*demonstrable, but even proven, he accepted the task of lecturing on*
*atheism to other members of the Soviet armed forces. But the*
*literature he studied to help him convince others that God did not*
*exist began to raise questions in his own mind. His doubts about God*
*were so strong that not one - or two - but THREE seemingly*
*miraculous answers to prayers to God were necessary before*
*Alexander was prepared to accept that what he had previously*
*believed, professed, and taught had been wrong.*

*In some ways Alexander's new life after he became a Christian*
*Believer was not easy either, at first within the Red Army, then outside*

*it. But Alexander testifies that knowing God personally has more than outweighed all the problems he had to overcome whilst living under a regime strongly opposed to the Christian Church, the Church's message, and every one of its individual members.*

*Today, Alexander is working alongside his wife, Svetlana, with the Slavic Gospel Association at SGA's International Headquarters in Loves Park, Illinois, USA, where the Editor first met them on one of his frequent visits in connection with the Radio Academy of Science. Alex now has special responsibility for modern media ministries - developing and implementing new ways of sharing the truth about God with both adults and children in Russia. In this chapter he explains how, against all the odds, he first found God for himself.*

Life for Christian Believers in the USSR was very tough. I witnessed many of their difficulties first-hand as a child, for several of my family were active in the Russian Orthodox Church. Some relatives were even deacons in it. Maybe the evident problems of belonging to any church in those days helped convince me in my teens that Christianity was definitely not for me! For example, few church buildings were open for worship; the numbers of services were strictly controlled by the Ministry of Cults; Bibles were rarely more than two per parish - one padlocked in the church, and one out of common reach in the priest's home; other Christian books were virtually non-existent; meetings for Believers in their own homes were forbidden, and teaching children about God was illegal; indeed, to profess faith in God oneself could be a recipe for disaster at school or work; and fines, family partition, imprisonment, or even exile to some distant labour camp threatened anyone considered to have erred in one or more of these respects.

But there were also other, more personal, reasons why I was not involved in any church activities: above all, I did not believe in the existence of the God whom Christians said they worshipped! Nothing we were taught in school admitted even a tiny possibility that God might be real; on the contrary, our frequent lessons in atheism insisted He was not. Furthermore, we were taught in Science that this key discipline incontrovertibly affirmed that the Universe, and all life in it, were just chance material phenomena which had developed spontaneously, without the aid of any 'creator' Being. So convinced did I become that the spiritual realm was a fantasy that I myself was soon teaching atheism to others, as an officer in the Soviet Army.

Certainly by nature I was disposed to straightforward explanations for everything. My natural tendency to pragmatism had been a decisive factor in my choice of career: on leaving school I had trained for five years to become an *"Engineer of Civil and Industrial Construction"*. The built environment is something we can design and relatively closely control. Yes, buildings are subject to vagaries of the environment, but through building standards and codes of practice even these can be quantified, and provisions made for them in respect of all but the rarest circumstances. Such power and precision appealed to my personal way of thinking: I had little time, and no affection, for *mysteries*!

At first, few mysteries were involved in my work for the Red Army. Much of this was concerned with the construction of an Air Force base, required for the defence of a strategic railroad. The rest of my duties revolved around my lectures on atheism. But, totally unexpectedly, it was in connection with these lecturing duties that things soon began to change. I was serious about my responsibilities as a lecturer, and decided that I should read as widely as possible about my subject. And the more I read, the more I came to think that there might just be a God after all!

Three books in particular began to shake my previously rigid thinking. Two were by a Polish author: one was called *"The Saga of the Evangelists"*, and the other simply *"Bible Stories"*. Both appealed to me because they were very objective, but both disturbed me because they presented arguments for, as well as against, the existence of God, and the authenticity of the Bible as literature inspired by God Himself.

Then a third book upset my preconceptions even more: this was the *"New Testament"* section of the Bible itself, a copy of which I discovered whilst searching for good atheistic material. The more I read the New Testament, the more deeply I began to question my firmly held anti-religious beliefs, indeed I even began to wonder if the Bible might be true. However, doubts continued to dominate my thinking in this area. Indeed, looking back, I have to say, very unreasonably so! In the New Testament we read of a man called Thomas, one of the followers of Jesus Christ. Thomas was particularly slow to accept that the miracle of Jesus rising from the dead three days after His crucifixion confirmed that Jesus had been God in a human form: Thomas had to literally feel for himself the wounds in the body of the resurrected Jesus before he was prepared to accept that this person was really Jesus. His doubts finally and conclusively laid to rest, Thomas collapsed in awe and shame at the feet of Jesus, crying out *"My Lord, and my God!"*

In a way I was to become an even greater doubter than Thomas, for I had to witness not *one* miracle, but THREE before I was to cast aside my own doubts concerning who Jesus was!

Somewhat ironically I took one decisive step away from my disbelief the day I voiced my doubts about the existence and power of God to the pastor of a local church I had begun to attend. *"If you want to be one hundred percent sure God exists, you must put Him to the test!"*, he replied, *"Try this now!"* At that time my mother was incurably ill. So I prayed to God *"If You are real, please cure my mother!"*

Soon, to my astonishment, doctors pronounced her cured!

I should have been convinced by this answer to prayer, but I thought this might have been just a happy coincidence: one miracle had not been enough, and my doubts remained.

Meanwhile, during this period my own health was not very good: I suffered frequently from asthma and bronchitis, and especially through the severe Siberian winters these illnesses slowed me down a lot. One day I seemed prompted to pray *"Please God, if You are real, cure me!"*

And He did this too! My health quickly improved! But two miracles were still not enough. Some of my doubts remained.

During that period we were building the rocket warehouse at the new air-base. This work was considered urgent, and we were often outdoors all day on it, even in the most extreme winter weather. Somehow the cold damaged my knee, indeed so badly and painfully that I could not walk. A Christian friend in the church I had been attending more and more, often prayed for my recovery: it was instantaneous! The whole congregation was very excited by this, but no-one more so than me! Three miracles were enough, even for 'Doubting Alexander': I could not doubt God any longer!

I was now sure, completely sure, that God was real, and wanted me to believe and trust in Him. Just as I had once strongly doubted God, now I strongly believed in Him, completely, without reservation. My inner turmoil over, I began to discover the peace of mind and soul I had come to want so much. More and more I came to appreciate and enjoy these and other *"mysteries of God's grace"* as my new found Christian friends described them, benefits which can be shared by all who ask God for His help in their lives.

However, as wonderful new spheres of knowledge and experience began to open up, so inevitably new problems began to afflict my life. Although my friends and I were careful not to talk openly about either my Christian conversion or my subsequent baptism, the military authorities became understandably suspicious when I told them I no longer wished to lecture in atheism. At first I gave no reasons for this, but was not really surprised when I was summoned to a 'conversation' with a group of KGB officers. In reality this was a detailed and forceful interrogation into my new personal beliefs, which were becoming increasingly obvious through changes in the way I behaved: I was now quieter, more self-controlled and responsible than I had been before. As times passed, the questioning became more and more intense. *"Why have you become a Christian Believer?"* my inquisitor wanted to know.... *"Who are members of the local church?"*.... *"Do Christians such as you in the military have any connections with churches in the West?"*

The implications of such questions were crystal clear: Christian Believers were not tolerated in the military forces of the USSR; Christians were not to be trusted; and action against them was necessary.

When the KGB realised the strength of my new faith they prompted my dismissal from the Red Army. This took effect in March 1985. But my problems were by no means over, for the local civilian authorities then took up the hunt. One way this manifested itself concerned my living accommodation: I tried to change my apartment for one in another city, but was not allowed to do so. Worse was to follow: I was ejected from my apartment, and given nowhere else to live. So I moved to Tashkent, 3000 kilometres away, where my mother had gone to live. I took a job as a labourer, because I thought that in a tough job like that I would not be hounded so much. Even so, the pressures brought to bear on me because I had come to believe in God were so strong that I eventually felt I had to leave my Mother Country altogether, and seek greater freedom to worship God, and share my knowledge of Him with others, in some other place.

Despite all the problems of such persecution, plus the continuing pain of separation from my home and many members of my family, I could never again doubt, ignore or neglect God: He is the One who has given real meaning and purpose to my life: He is the One who has given me unprecedented peace and happiness even in the most difficult of circumstances. Now I know God personally I can say it is the most logical thing of all to trust Him completely, at all times, and in every way. I strongly recommend you to trust Him too, however high the cost may seem to be. God is described in the Bible as *"no-one's debtor"*. Knowing Him and the warmth of His love is more than recompense for any persecution we could ever suffer for being known to live for Him!

# 9.

# From Frustration to Freedom

**Josef Chaplar**
(*Evangelist, Györ, Hungary*)

**Josef Chaplar** *knows a lot about* frustration. *First and foremost he was a frustrated agricultural scientist. From early childhood he always* "wanted to be studying subjects that answered the question 'WHY?' " *and enjoyed his course when a student of Animal Breeding and Husbandry at the Agricultural Academy in the Hungarian town of Mosonmagyaróvár. However, the Communist ideology which was being imposed on Hungary at that time did not always permit such a question to be answered objectively, and when the political uprising of 1956 was forcibly put down by the Russian army, Josef knew it was personally prudent to escape to the West as a refugee. Whilst this was the gateway to greater personal freedom, the need to work, and learn a new language, frustrated his strong ambitions to study systematically and research more.*

*From refugee camps in Austria Josef lost the opportunity (on account of a drinking spree!) to emigrate to the USA, and moved on, virtually by accident, to England instead. There he settled, and married, only to suffer the disappointments and frustrations of limited qualifications, a broken marriage, and ill health. Things began to improve after he met his present wife, Wendy. Then she, and he, began to discover really satisfying answers to the "Why?" questions he had still been asking: in 1985 he began to forget his frustrations, found God personally, and, for the first time in his life, felt really free.*

*Today, despite Josef's earlier total lack of desire to return to the country of his birth and youth, Josef and Wendy are serving God together in Hungary. Josef is an ordained Evangelist in the north west of the country, based in the regional capital, Györ. It was here that the Editor, after participating in an international scientific conference in Budapest, first met the Chaplars, and began to learn of their desire to share their relatively new-found faith with others, especially young people.*

*Today, Josef is happy.* "I used to think Science could solve every problem", *he says.* "I needed to believe that the more we discovered, the better we should be able to live! But when I found the Lord, and began walking with Him, I started to see both Science and mankind in different ways. And I now know that it is only when God enters our lives that everything can begin to make real sense."

———————

I was born in a district of Budapest in 1935. My family was one of the many in Hungary which had been noble, but had been left only with their pride. So, to make ends meet, my father and grandfather had become master painter/decorators. It was my grandmother who was most proud of our ancestry, and during the first part of World War II, I moved to live with her in Györ, in her ancestral home. This was a long house with many rooms, huge beamed ceilings, and big gardens.

My grandmother taught me to read and write when I was very young, but I never read many children's books. At home, and at school in the St. Benedictine monastery a few kilometres away at Pannonhalma, I was brought up on serious stories, and to study and discuss things seriously. This meant that I never managed to develop the kind of small talk considered polite in high society, and I always wanted to study subjects answering the question *"Why?"* This curiosity lead me to look at all sorts of problems: for example how our bodies work, and what makes us and animals behave the way they do. I also wanted to understand how I, as a living being, fitted into the world as a whole. However I found the response of others frustrating, for adults didn't always take me seriously, and other kids weren't interested in my questions.

When the time came to move on to higher education, I felt drawn to Physical Science, or Electronics. But my grandmother said gentlemen didn't study things like that: I must study Forestry or nothing at all! By then, though, the Communist Party was in power in Hungary, and as in many areas of life, they made the decision for me. I was sent to the Agricultural Academy at Mosonmagyaróvár. Fortunately, my curiosity helped me enjoy my studies, especially questions like how plants and animals are different, why one animal is black and another brown, and why one grain of wheat is bigger than another. I also became interested in Sociology and Politics: why some people have more to live on than others, and how things could be made more balanced for everyone.

To gain some practical experience as part of my higher level studies, I was sent to a very large state-owned agricultural station. At this time the collective farm system was being pressed on the farmers by the government, and one of my jobs was to try to encourage independent farmers to join collectives. However, I could see that the system was based on ideology, not market forces, or even commonsense. The system was for the system alone, not for the people. It was ridiculous for the government to insist on a Five-Year Plan that ignored the local soil type, or the animals you had! Often equipment that wasn't needed was supplied, and equipment that was needed was unavailable. But officials would complain if the Plan was not being fulfilled, and farmers had to try to grow crops they knew would not succeed in a particular area. Personally, I did not believe the collective farm system was sensible - so I often told farmers how they could avoid entering it....!

After a short time I was told to move to a large mixed Experimental State Farm on the Austro-Hungarian border. I found this farm much more interesting. One of its concerns was the development of better seeds. Another concern - and one I particularly enjoyed - was animal breeding. This was not for work or slaughter, but for special purposes. We bred pigs for a laboratory producing serums, and cows for studies of feed additives to improve milk yields. We were also trying to create herds of cattle that were free from diseases, including tuberculosis and brucellosis. I was particularly interested in twin calves, measuring and analysing them to decide whether they were from a single cell or not. We had little access to scientific papers or results from elsewhere - none at all from the West, though a little was beginning to come from the Soviet Union. Mostly we had to work out the effects of genetics for ourselves.

During that period my interests in the political system and problems of ordinary people continued to grow, but we all had to be careful what we said and did! A Communist Party Secretary was based on the farm. He crept around, listening at doors and windows. Although illiterate, he posed a lot of problems. Many of my colleagues were taken away for questioning, and some never returned. Being so close to the Austrian border we could see the other side, and a kind of life totally different from ours. Many folk tried to escape to it, though many failed! At night we would hear gunfire, or explosions in the border minefields. Often in the morning I would see someone hanging on the border barbed wire, where he or she had been shot the night before. I grew more and more depressed by the ways our lives were controlled, as if in a prison.

Then, in 1956, just as I was due to return to the Academy in Mosonmagyaróvár for more advanced studies, there was revolution, with fighting in cities all across Hungary including Budapest, of course, but in Mosonmagyaróvár also, where troops opened fire on the crowds. I was most upset, for many of my college friends were killed. Being on the border with Austria, some of us helped more and more of the people who were coming through, trying to escape before the Russians could close the frontier completely. We gave the fugitives food, and fuel for their vehicles. We were very well placed to help: I myself had permits which allowed me to go up to the border wire itself. But, one night, a group we were waiting to help didn't arrive. If any of that group had been caught and interrogated, my name might have emerged! So I decided I had to escape too.

Looking back, I admit there was some cowardice in my decision, but that's how it was. Finding the route wasn't difficult because I know the borders as well as any border guard. It was rainy, as it had been for several days. The fields were ploughed because it was Autumn. I went some way on horseback, then let the horse go and proceeded on foot. As I approached the border itself I had to lie in the mud for a while as patrols passed. Then I had a decision to make: should I *walk carefully* across the minefield, knowing some mines had been detonated, but others had not.... or should I *run* across as quickly as possible?! Being a good runner, and being afraid of being seen and shot, I did the 100 metres sprint, running as quickly as possible whilst wearing riding boots, and soaking wet from head to toe. Just as I reached the Austrian side there was a commotion behind me, so I dropped down behind some maize piled ready for collection.

For a long while I couldn't move! I think that the fear of being shot or blown up had caught up with me. At long last the noise died down, and I was able to set off towards the village of Nickelsdorf. I was free, both from political oppression, and immediate personal danger. But it would be a long time before I would be free from the effects of my own sinful life, or from deepening personal frustration. I walked into the village police station and said simply *"Here I am!"*

      *             *             *             *

Although I was not really aware of it at the time - for everything seemed so unreal - several things happened in Austria which were to radically affect the rest of my life. The first was a matter of the *heart*. After being kept in a church hall in Nickelsdorf for a few days a group of us were moved to a larger refugee camp in Wiener Neustadt. I had spent a lot of time in the village back in Hungary dancing with a girl I fancied. Her father came looking for her, thinking I had taken her away with me. I had not, and realised I would probably never see her again....!

Then there were matters of *country* and *career*. I found refugee life quite interesting, being taken to new places, and meeting new people. After being moved twice more, into the Austria Tyrol, I found myself in a large ex-French army camp with over 5000 other Hungarian refugees. We talked a lot, and I began thinking in which country I would like to live now I had some choice. Australia was one possibility, but so too was the USA. I filled out a 25-page form for emigration to the United States, and was told *"OK, you can go there!"*

But I didn't! The buses to take us on the first stage of the journey were late, so some of us went to the nearby inn. By the time the transport came we had had enough beers to say *"The buses can go; we are staying here: we'll be alright!"* Life continued as before in the camp, until representatives came to tell us how wonderful life was in the French Foreign Legion. I decided to join it, but when the Camp Commander heard about this, for some reason he was very angry, and I learned some Hungarian words I had never heard before! *"There is a train leaving tomorrow for England"* he barked *"BE ON IT!"* So, after a quick interview and finger printing, it was onto that train. Within 24 hours we had arrived at Ostend and were put on a boat for Dover. That's how, for better or for worse, I arrived in the UK, penniless, and with no knowledge of the English language....

\*                    \*                    \*                    \*

On the cross-Channel steamer we had our first English breakfast, of bacon, egg, toast etc., and the interpreter said that the English were rejoicing to be able to welcome us. So we felt good - though when we landed at Dover we didn't see any welcome at all on the faces of the dockers! But we were there - with more new experiences to follow! After an all night train journey we were taken by double decker bus to a Royal Air Force camp in Lincolnshire. It was my first time on a 'double decker', and upstairs it swayed around so much I felt not only tired, but also sick.

New frustrations I came to experience were even worse than those before, because they were longer lived. I wanted to study in a university, but learned that they had already filled their Hungarian refugee student quotas. Since I did not speak any English, I was very restricted in the work I could do. Needing work of any kind I could get, I agreed to work on a farm. Some farmers came to select 10 of us from a group of 60. Since none of the farmers spoke Hungarian, they walked us past them and pointed to the ones they thought looked best. *"Well"*, I thought afterwards, *"At least this is different from being SENT to work on a farm: here I've been CHOSEN!"*

At first I found the different farming methods interesting. I also liked the English beer, and dancing. But I soon became more frustrated than I had ever been before, because there was nothing I could read. So I began to teach myself to read English, at first through comics. It was a slow process, and the first two years in England were a desperate time for me, and my loneliness was sometimes quite terrifying.

Over the years that followed I moved from one place and one job to another. Most were menial jobs, including killing chickens on a poultry farm, and labouring on building sites. I wasn't always truthful at my interviews: when I went for one job as a steam crane driver in a foundry I said I used to do that in Hungary. I got the job, but when they said *"Get on with it!"* I had to say *"This engine is different from the ones in Hungary!"* So they had to show me how to drive it! I enjoyed more a job with Pedigree Pet Foods, because there was more science in the problems of how the materials behaved, and how they had to be worked to get the shapes we wanted.

The search for work had led me to the town of Melton Mowbray in Leicestershire. And it was there that a game of soccer in the street with two little boys of six and seven led me to meet their mother, a widow for two years. *"Mum says you can come in for tea if you want to"* they said. So I did, and soon married her! We had a son of our own called Adrian, but I loved all the boys. After 16 years my wife and I agreed to part company, on friendly terms. I had had to give up work because of a chronic eye complaint, and wanted to study more, maybe with the Open University through a postal course, but my wife had given me no encouragement to do this.

At last, with time to spare, after nearly 30 years in England, I decided to learn English more formally. Through the local Adult Literacy Centre I met a tutor called Wendy. She had had marriage difficulties too, and was separated from her husband and two children. After a while we decided to live together, and felt happier. Then God began to speak to us, and true happiness, and real freedom, were just around the corner at long last.

Wendy's daughter, Rachael, suddenly said she would like to go to church. Wendy began going with her, first to one church, then to Melton Mowbray Baptist Church. One day they came home and said they had become Christians! I said *"Big deal! If you live in England, of course you're Christians!"* But they said *"No, it's not like that at all!"* It was obvious, too, that something had happened to them. *They* kept smiling, and being happy; *I* became more and more angry because of it! After they left for church on Sunday morning, I would go to the pub. But I felt increasingly uncomfortable about this situation and one Sunday, when Wendy got up, I did so too, and began to dress. *"What are you doing?"* she asked. When I said *"I'm coming to church too"* she started to cry!

I was perplexed: I was wrong not to go to church, but made Wendy cry if I said I would! Whatever I did seemed to be wrong. I guess I had never seen tears of joy before.

Entering the church I was greeted by Fred Clark. Fred has been a leader there for over 40 years, always welcoming people to the meetings. He held his hand out to me and said *"Welcome, brother!"*

That was the first time in my life I had felt someone had been happy to see me in spite of not knowing anything about me. Inside the church I found surprises too. The church I had been taken to as a child in Hungary had been quiet and dimly-lit, and the people very formal with each other. Now, in Melton Mowbray, it impressed me that in this church people were greeting each other happily, even with embraces and kisses, though when the singing began, with choruses, and arms raised, I thought it was just not proper! Then a guy I had known for some time went up to preach. He was the Baptist minister, and as he preached about Job and all his suffering I kept thinking *"Why is he looking at me, and preaching to me, when there are 200 other people in the church?"* But I kept going there, and gradually I found I was receiving answers to many of my old questions including *"Who am I?"* and *"Why am I here?"*, and many of my old frustrations began to seem very unimportant.

One day, when I was alone at home thinking about all these things, I came to the point where I just said *"Well, Jesus, if you really are everything people say you are, here I am, do something about ME!"*

The change He made in me was very sudden, and dramatic. I no longer wanted to spend time drinking beer, but I wanted to know more about the Bible. I didn't have to worry about my previously long unanswered questions, for God is the One Who has the answers. I didn't have to rack my brain about how to change either myself or the way society works, for God has everything in His hands. Mankind has been making great progress with scientific discoveries, and creating everything from non-stick saucepans to the Space Shuttle, but we have been losing our sense of the mysterious, and denying the miraculous. I realised more and more that the only satisfactory answers to all our questions about life and its purpose are given by God the Father, through the Lord Jesus Christ, Who is our way to Him. I felt, and was, really free at last!

All this was very radical for me. So, too, were the consequences! When I had come to England in 1957 I had said I would never go to church again, but there I was going to church, and liking it, and knowing God myself. Also, I had said I would never go to Hungary again. But one Sunday I felt God was telling me to go back there. At first I was very reluctant even to think about this. Hungary was still under communist rule, and I had had no contact with anyone there for over 30 years. But God blesses us when we are obedient to Him, and I planned a visit. At the Hungarian border my fear was just as bad as when I had crossed it before, that night in 1956. But then I realised everything was different: *I was in the hand of God.* In Budapest I met with fellow Christian Believers, and on returning to England said to my wife (Wendy and I had, of course, married by then!), *"Well, I think I have to go back again!"*

Needing the kind of job I could get away from sometimes, I started a transport business, and began to travel widely in Eastern Europe to encourage Christians, in Russia and The Ukraine as well as Hungary itself. Wendy and I were really being blessed by God. He had convicted us of all the sins in our lives, the consequences of living without Him. Now He had forgiven us, everything we had, and thought we should do, was brought before Him. So we had this great new life we were slowly building. The business was a problem, though, because it became more important than we had wanted. The time came when someone said to Wendy and myself *"You two are never together nowadays! Why don't you have a holiday? I will pay for you to go to the Keswick Convention!"* We had a lovely time at this great annual event, a week of Christian meetings in the Lake District of north-western England, worshipping with thousands of others in the enormous tent, and listening to good preachers and teachers.

In the middle of the week, at the end of the Missionary Meeting, the leader asked *"Is there anybody who feels God is calling them to missionary service?"* Wendy got up and went to the front, and I just followed her. Our counsellor, the international evangelist Luis Palau, said *"You're already spending most of your time in Eastern Europe. That's your mission field!"* So we packed our belongings into an old van and set off for Hungary. At first I still kept my business, thinking I still had to provide for us so that the Lord would have some of our time to use. But the business began to get in the way, so I sold it - although I have never been *paid* for it! We have been through many testing times since then, but the Lord has, in different ways, provided everything we've needed, and has blessed all we have done. It has been a story of one blessing after another.

Today I work in north-western Hungary, as an ordained evangelist of the Hungarian Baptist Union. Churches there are growing, and new ones being started. People are open to the Gospel, and want to hear it. It is our privilege to be able to take it to them.

*                    *                    *                    *

So my life has changed completely. It is great to be free *personally*, and to live a normal life not only in England, but in Hungary too now this is governed democratically. But it is even better to be free *spiritually*, free from sin, and the guilt that goes with it. And it is wonderful to be free *mentally* from all the frustrations I had because I couldn't study properly for a career in Science, and to know where God wants us to be today.

I'm still interested in Science, but I see it now in a different way. Science has achieved so much, but is not leading people to better lives.

More physical comforts are being provided by technology, but spiritual misery and pain are growing. God was and is the real starting point for everything, but more and more He is being neglected. Many scientists are pursuing Science not as a way of honouring Him, but as an end in itself. So this becomes more and more of a treadmill, because every time Science finds an answer for anything, many more questions are thrown up. And people become depressed when they find that their new discoveries don't bring either fulfilment or satisfaction. They don't bring them nearer God! So I have learnt that the most important thing in the world is our relationship with God. He is the answer to our deeper needs. Finding Him for ourselves is the best and most valuable discovery we could ever make.

In my lifetime, I have seen a major war, and the tragedy it brought. I have seen the effects of dictatorship, and of communism. I have lived through a revolution, and seen people kill for seemingly no reason at all. I have lived in refugee camps and have seen perfectly normal men and women behaving in ways they themselves would never have believed possible: men stealing, women prostituting themselves to feed their children, and girls prostituting themselves from sheer boredom. I went to live in a foreign country without knowing a word of its language, and took any job I could to earn a living, lacking real identity and feeling neither truly British nor truly Hungarian.

Not surprisingly I was, as an unbeliever, angry with God - if He existed! Rather, I hoped instead that Science would solve every problem, but increasingly recalled the Biology lesson at school which concerned a frog. At first it was alive, hopping, and seeming happy. The teacher then killed and dissected it. I remember thinking at the end of the lesson that we knew a lot more about the frog than at the beginning - but now *the frog was dead*! Today my greatest concern is this: just as I used to be God-less, and therefore spiritually dead in my sins, so are most other people today. They may know many things, but unless they know God, *their souls are dead*. And what value is there in a living body, and an understanding mind, if the soul is dead? It has been my greatest joy to find God, and get to know Him. It is now my responsibility to help others find Him also, especially young people with past problems, meaningless presents, and empty futures.

I believe that it is the responsibility of *all* scientists who are Christians to bring Science and God back together. He is central to everything, the answer to the most important questions we can ask. Modern Science began with Theology, considering our position relative to God's. We need to return to that point, for we are God's creation, spiritual creatures who, without Him, are incomplete. It doesn't matter whatever we do for our bodies if our spirits are living in misery, crying out for God! And I know that, just as God has changed my life so completely, and given me real peace and purpose, so He can change and bless others too.

# 10.

## TIME TO THINK

**Ann Barnett**
(*Computer Consultant, Nairobi, Kenya*)

**Ann Barnett** *is unique amongst the scientists featured in this book: whereas almost all are known by the Editor, and have told their personal stories to him, Ann is the only one who has been one of his students. Born and brought up in the east African republic of Kenya, Ann works today with a major multinational computer company, mostly in Africa but revisiting the United Kingdom from time to time on business. And it was in the UK previously that Ann studied for her Bachelor of Science Honours Degree, spending three years as an undergraduate in the Editor's academic department in the University of Bristol. Dr. Barrett became impressed with the unusually questioning mind Ann Barnett has.... and Ann herself was impressed when she learnt that this scientist, lecturing to her class in Climatology, and Environmental Remote Sensing, courses has a deep and active Christian faith.*

*On her own confession, Ann is a* "very competitive person". *In her teens, she not only studied hard at her school in Nairobi, but also played hard, at a variety of sports. A particularly gifted swimmer, she represented Kenya several times in this sport, culminating in a number of individual and relay events in the All-Africa Games.*

*Unfortunately, such a full life left Ann with little time to think about spiritual things. It was not until her university student days in*

*Bristol that she felt she really wanted to find out if there was a God....*
*and, if so, whether this fact had any special relevance for her as an*
*individual.*

*The following conversation took place just before Ann left Bristol*
*after her Graduation Day.*

---

Editor:    Ann, there are clearly many things we could discuss at the
           end of your studies in Bristol - especially the things that
           surprised you, or did not work out the way you expected.
           But, as you know, I am a Christian Believer, and I know you
           have come to be one too whilst you have been here with us.
           So what I want to discover most of all is this: how have you
           come to faith in God?

Ann:       You are right about the surprises, for there have been many of
           them!  But most of all I would never have expected that I
           would be leaving Bristol not only with a degree, but also a
           real live faith in Jesus Christ!

           Perhaps I could begin by saying why I had not become a
           Christian earlier?

Editor:    I am sure that would be very interesting!

Ann:       *One* reason was that I was not brought up in a Christian
           home.  It was certainly a loving, caring home - but my parents
           have never been church goers.  Encouraged by my great-
           grandmother, I went to Sunday School for some years when I
           was really young.  I enjoyed it, and was interested in the
           Bible stories I heard.  But we never discussed Christian
           things at home, so I left them behind in church.  Through all
           this period the Christian message did not really penetrate my
           mind.

           A *second* reason why I did not become a Christian earlier was
           that it was not fashionable to be a Christian in the European
           community in Kenya!  The native churches there are always
           full, but very few white people in Kenya go to church.  Many
           have a rather tough way of life, lubricated by large quantities
           of alcoholic drinks!  As I grew older, and entered my teens, I
           began to think that Christianity was dull, old-fashioned, and

much too restrictive to appeal to me in any way at all.

Of course, I knew some Europeans who were Christians, but most of them were missionaries or from missionary families. I resented them because they seemed to be changing the traditional lifestyles of the native Africans. Missionaries were often blamed for things which were not their fault, like the economic exploitation of the blacks. I did have some missionary friends who were very nice indeed - but I told myself they were the exceptions, and generally believed the unfair publicity most missionaries were given.

My *third* reason for not becoming a Christian earlier was that I got too busy with school work and sport to have time to think seriously about spiritual things. Hillcrest Secondary School in Nairobi is not only very multiracial - there are European pupils, as well as Africans, Americans and Asians - but also a high-pressure place. The Asians were especially hardworking students. I have always been a very competitive kind of person, so I worked hard to try to beat them.

So it did not seem to me, as a budding environmental scientist, that Christianity could provide the answer to any questions that really mattered.

Editor:     You say you are a very competitive person. This personal characteristic has been rewarded in the swimming pool, but I guess your swimming took a lot of your time too?

Ann:        Absolutely! I worked really hard to get into the Kenyan national team! But I was keen on almost every other sport you can think of too. And the successes I enjoyed in many of those areas of my life added to the reasons for not even *wanting* to become a Christian!

Editor:     Well, I know you are a Christian now, so things must have changed dramatically after you came to Bristol! Tell us what happened then.

Ann:        I said that one reason I did not become a Christian earlier was because I could not discuss spiritual questions with my family. In Bristol I soon found lots of students eager to discuss such things. Like my mother, I had been prepared to believe in some vague 'higher power' in the Universe. Now I began to feel I wanted to find out if there truly was a God - and if I could know Him in some way myself.

I made friends with some great students in my year in our University department - Julia, Graham and Megan especially - somewhat coincidentally, all tutorial students of yours! Previously, I would have shied away from Christianity, largely through ignorance. Now I began to learn from my new friends what it is really like, and I began to realise it is well worth having. Then, when I went home to Kenya in the vacations, I found more super Christians there too. So, for the first time in my life I began thinking - and talking - about spiritual things, both deeply and seriously.

Editor:   You said one reason why Christianity had not appealed to you earlier was because it had seemed stuffy and out-of-date. How did you discover that true Christianity is not like this at all?

Ann:      Mainly through what I saw in people whom I knew were Believers in Jesus Christ. Jane was one of these. She was training to be a teacher. She had already got a First Class Honours degree in Chemistry from Nottingham University. Now, as you know very well, First Class degrees are very hard to get! But Jane was not only an excellent scholar: she was talented at everything - yet was still great fun to be with. Since she is a great person in every way, you will understand when I say how impressed I was to discover she is a Christian!

          Then I discovered that you are a Christian too. It impressed me even more to think that some of my *professors* were Christians! I had not thought Christianity and Science were compatible. Now I knew that they must be so.

Editor:   They are indeed! But tell us next how, at last, you made time to search for God yourself at University. Your personal schedule must have been even busier than it had been at Hillcrest School in Nairobi!

Ann:      I guess we all make time to do the things we think are really vital! At first, as I began to recognize my need of God, I would go into churches just to sit and think. I found them restful and relaxing places.

          Then my friend Megan introduced me to the leader of a so-called 'Basics' group in the University. These groups are for people who want to discuss fundamental spiritual questions, and find the answers to them. Through these discussions I began to realize that God must indeed be real - and wanted even me to reach out to Him. I wanted to find out more about Him, so I made more time to go to helpful meetings like those!

An old and favourite misconception of mine had been the belief that *"Christians are the only people who NEED Christianity!"* I began to realise that *everyone* needs a Christian faith. And that included me!

Editor:  On a very personal note, I must say that we have rarely had a student in our Department who has been so keen to ask questions about her academic work as you have been! So, knowing you as I do, I am sure you proceeded to consider spiritual questions very thoroughly, too!

Ann:    You are right, I did! And, gradually, I came to understand that God is not just a mysterious 'higher power' distinguished by a special name of His own. I began to see that He is a great, awe-inspiring Being - but, at the same time, One Who also cares for me as an individual person! Soon after this I found I could communicate with Him myself, in prayer.

But the real turning point in my life came about four months ago, when I asked Him to take control of my life, and help me live it in a way which would please Him. Since then I have discovered God to be a very personal friend, a helper, a guardian in difficult circumstances. One with Whom I can share everything in my life! You know, I have always been a very independent sort of person, but I have now submitted myself to God as Lord of everything I am and do. And I am so glad I have!

Before I came to know God myself, one thing I had already come to realize was that Christians have a special quality about them. I guess the chief thing is their sense of *inner peace*. That frustrated me, because it was something I did not understand. But now I do - and God is giving me this peace too. I thank Him for it every day. It is so important to say *"thank you"* to Him for everything!

Editor:  That is a great testimony to the way God works - and what He does! There is no doubt there has been a real change in you, and in your life: I have seen it very clearly. But let me ask you one last question: how do you now see Science in relation to Christianity?

Ann:    One thing my course of studies in this Department has made me realize is that Science is more *subjective* than many people think. Like Christianity, it depends a lot on the faith and experience of the individual.

But the other thing I should say is that it is possible to be much more *objective* in choosing to test the Christian faith than many people think. True, Christianity involves the emotions, but it also challenges - and satisfies - the intellect! I am glad I discovered this faith for myself at University. Here we are attuned to be receptive to new ideas, yet trained to treat each one critically. I approached the Christian faith this way, thinking a lot about it before trying it myself. Then I decided very positively that faith in God was worth the test, and it was then that I found that it really WORKS! And I feel I can make much more of my faith because of this critical way I have come to it than if I had grown up with it from childhood.

In some ways I want now to emulate our African gardener, Ambede, at home in Nairobi. He is a fine Christian, pure and cheerful. He always speaks of the importance of doing everything in God's name. I have not been used to thinking like that myself. Indeed, I used to think this philosophy of his was too good to be true! But now I want Ambede to become one - excellent - model for my new life as a Christian. I am looking forward to going home shortly and telling him that I have become a Christian too.

Editor:  Thank you, Ann, for taking us along this personal path of yours to faith in God. I am sure Ambede will be delighted to hear this story.... but he could not be more pleased to hear it than I myself have been!

Over the years in which I have been a university professor I have watched many students - at least temporarily - *lose* their faith in God, usually because this was something they had grown up with at home, and which was therefore neither firmly founded on their own understanding of the Christian gospel, nor the result of a conscious choice their own.

But I have also seen others who, like you, have *found* faith in

God at university: faith which is all the more strong and secure because it is the result of critical thought, and a conscious, personal search for the greatest truths of life and the Universe. I am sure that, in the years ahead, this new faith of yours will be of much greater value to you than your degree!

# 11.

## PROGRESSIVE LEARNING

**Andrew Chadwick**
*(Senior School Master, Bournemouth, England)*

*If you have read the earlier Chapter entitled "Personal Experiments" featuring Dr. David Chadwick, you will realise that the subject of this Chapter, **Andrew Chadwick** has the same family name. Indeed, David and Andrew are from the same immediate family, being brothers!*

*Like David, Andrew also studied Chemistry at degree level after leaving school, although in his case at the University of Aston in Birmingham, England. Unlike David, whom (you may remember!) needed 'time-fillers' in research, and abroad, until he found which career he really wanted to follow, Andrew did not undertake research after his Bachelor of Science degree. Instead, being certain he wanted to become a secondary school teacher, Andrew took a one-year Postgraduate Certificate in Education course to qualify him for the teaching profession in the UK. He then went on to teach at Ferndown School near Bournemouth, on the south coast of England, and has been there ever since.*

*The Editor met Andrew Chadwick a few years ago, after Andrew had become engaged to marry. For Deborah, his fiancee, was a nurse who, through her training in Bristol and frequent visits to the Barrett home, had become a close friend of this family, It began to emerge that Andrew has clear thoughts on vital parts of the education*

*process.... and that Andrew had followed a 'progressive learning' path*
*in his personal search for a solution to the 'deep dissatisfaction' he*
*said he had long felt with himself and with his life.  Indeed, there had*
*come a point at which, Andrew confesses,* "If I had not been a coward,
I would have committed suicide!" *These interrelated matters are*
*explored in the pages which follow: like almost all the other Chapters*
*of this book, this one has been up-dated from a script originally*
*prepared for the Radio Academy of Science series of broadcasts.*

---

Editor:    Andrew, you always wanted to become a school teacher, and
           you have now gained many years experience of teaching
           Science.   First, let us talk a little about *methods and*
           *philosophies* of teaching.  Would we be right in thinking that
           there are probably different kinds of scientific knowledge
           which are appropriate for students at different educational
           levels?

Andrew: Yes, you are right!

Editor:    Then does this fact have any practical effects on the way
           Chemistry is taught in schools and colleges?

Andrew: I would say it affects this very profoundly!  Take the case of
           my own school, at Ferndown.  This school caters for teenage
           children between the ages of 13 and 19.    The younger
           members of this age group come to us having had little or no
           formal training in my subject.   In the senior classes, the
           students have some choice of the curricula they follow.  I'm
           sorry to say, relatively few choose to study Chemistry, for the
           assumption is that those who do study it at senior school level
           are likely to go on to read for a degree involving Chemistry at
           university.  Now these three levels - introductory, advanced,
           and degree level - involve not only different *amounts* of
           knowledge, but also different *types* of knowledge.  I think this
           is probably true of many other scientific disciplines too.

Editor:    Can you give us an example of the different types of
           information involved in Chemistry, and how these are taught?

Andrew: In Chemistry - as you may remember from your own
           schooldays - attention is focussed on substances, or

'chemicals'.... especially chemicals which figure importantly in everyday life. One such group of substances consists of the 'acids'. These affect us all, every day we live. *Hydrochloric acid* in our stomachs helps digest the food we eat; *sulphuric acid* helps provide the energy from car batteries which prompt our cars to start, and power their lights especially when they are parked in the dark; *several acids* together may be responsible for making soils fit or unfit for some types of plants we wish to grow in our gardens; *other acids* are washed out of the atmosphere as acid rain, damaging forests and buildings made of calcareous materials like limestone. The school syllabus I teach is structured so that the junior classes are taught mainly the *actions* of acids.... the senior classes are taught mainly the *properties* of acids.... and, at university, I recall, I was taught mainly the *reasons* for those different actions and properties of acids. There is, of course, some mixing, some overlap, between these things, but this is an example of how the emphases in Chemistry syllabi change as students become more knowledgeable.

Editor:  So the emphasis is, at first, on what acids *do*.... then on what acids *are*.... then on *how and why* they behave in such ways?

Andrew: You've got it right!

Editor:  So how does this progression work out in practice, through class-room teaching about acids?

Andrew: With my younger classes, I talk about, and demonstrate through simple experiments, the most distinctive things acids *do*.... like reacting with metals to produce hydrogen as a by-product.... reacting with bases to give salts.... and giving a red or orange colour when tested with an indicator solution, or a pink coloration to litmus paper.

With my more advanced classes I have to encourage the students to - as it were - get *inside* the acids, so as to understand their internal structures. So our attention turns more to how these compounds are built up by atoms of individual elements and, most importantly in the case of acids, how these particular chemicals all have one or more hydrogen atoms which are available to be replaced by others, for example by metals.

Then, at university level, I recall that our professors spent most time explaining in detail *why acids are so different* from all other chemicals.... We were taken all the way down to the sub-atomic level, and were introduced to the specific behaviour of the sub-microscopic particles which compose each acid.

Editor:   You suggested earlier that patterns of progressive learning are widespread in the sciences. Would you say that progressive learning is much more widespread than the example you have given?

Andrew: Yes, I am sure it is.

In fact, I can see the need for a similar learning progression not just in Science, but in most areas of life. For example, we discovered from our first baby, daughter Rebekah, that even very young children *watch what older people do*, and copy them! Next, it seems we have to teach infants *what things are*, so they can use them more fully. Then, like more advanced students, children begin to get interested in *how things work* and begin to bombard us for explanations - many of which, of course, we cannot provide!

And for us older folk such a progression applies not only to learning about chemicals and other things that have material substance. I see the material Universe as a framework within which much more exists, and much more happens. I am sure progressive learning really helps in these areas too! Let's turn from Science for a moment and consider *artistic creativity*. This is sometimes characterised as something which is either born in us, or not - but those who have it can still learn to use it better. Then there is *philosophical thought*. This, too, may come to us relatively easily, or it may not - but formal training in it helps enormously. And we must not forget *spiritual activity*, including awareness of God, and becoming spiritually alive.... This life is available to us all - but without conscious thought and progressive effort, we can miss out on it entirely: without care, and effort, we can miss out on the chief purpose, and the greatest pleasures, of life!

Editor:   Certainly there are many philosophical arguments which support the suggestion that the Universe is a spiritual, as well as a material, realm.... and that the supernatural spiritual being we call 'God' has created the physical Universe, and given us the physical life we possess. But what physical evidences do you see which confirm that the spiritual realm is real, and that God really does exist? If the physical and spiritual realms co-exist, as you have suggested, evidence of the spiritual realm often must be clear in the realm of the physical?

Put differently, perhaps the the most important question I can ask you is this: if, as you have implicitly suggested, we are not *born* with fully-developed spiritual awareness, is it possible for us to *train* our senses to ensure we do not miss out on - how did you put it again - *"the greatest pleasures of life"*?

Andrew: These are vast questions, and it would take a long time to answer them fully! But I can outline one way in which they can be answered. We spoke earlier about acids, and how people become educated about them. We saw that the progression is from learning about what they *do*, to what they *are*, and to *how and why* they are unique.

Then we talked about children learning about life, and how we may help facilitate and speed that process.

So far as education in *spiritual awareness* is concerned, perhaps my own experience will again serve as a useful model. It was in 1980 that my own life changed dramatically for the better. I suppose you could say that it was then that I was 'born again': it was in 1980 that I became not just physically, but also spiritually alive. In one sense this was a rather unexpected and very sudden happening. But in another it was just a sudden result of a process which had begun some considerable time before: the result of a lengthy period of progressive education about the spiritual realm - based almost entirely on what you have called 'physical evidences' that God is real! For me, these evidences most clearly sprang from the lives of Christians: people who had already come to know God for themselves.

At first, I began to notice what Christians *do*. Some of these things are quite obvious! For example, Christians go to church, they praise God together, read and study their Bibles, and pray. But other things they do were at first less obvious to me, and I did not begin to appreciate some of them until I approached my mid-teens. However, some of these things are at least equally important, and in some ways are even more informative about God and the Christian faith.

You see, despite all the negative propaganda, and popularity of cruel jokes about true Christians, I began to notice that as a group they were much kinder, and more genuinely unselfish, than the other people I knew. I recognized the genuine kindness of Christians most vividly when I was verbally abused by some of my school mates. You see, in my teens I was grossly overweight. I weighed more at ages 13 and 14 than I do now, in middle age! I was teased so much that, if I had not been a coward at heart, I would have committed suicide. I certainly thought more than once about this way of escape from the problems of my life. But some folk I knew to be Christians were sympathetic, and understanding. Maybe they even saved my life at that time.

After I had completed university and begun teaching, I thought if I helped others more I would cure the deep dissatisfaction I still felt with life. So I responded to an advertisement for spare-time voluntary work with a charitable organisation.

Unfortunately, as in the case of my brother David's voluntary work in Ghana, this did not satisfy my need either, although I did not understand why at the time.

However, it was through my voluntary work that I became increasingly aware of a group of people who were also helping others, but with a major difference: they were not helping others *to satisfy needs of their own*, but out of *genuine concern for the needs of others*. Little by little I learned that those extremely unselfish colleagues were Christian Believers too. I guess it was only then that I became aware not only of what Christians do, but of what Christians *are:* the second step in my personal spiritual education.

Very slowly I grew to understand that genuine followers of Christ were not only much happier and more content than I had ever been, but could also help others in a totally unselfish way, for this reason: they themselves had *no obvious unmet physical or spiritual needs*! This came to impress me, as did the deeply peaceful natures of these people: Christians seemed able to draw from sources of inner strength and stability quite outside my own experience and understanding. Fortunately, I went on to discover, too, that Christians do not want to make secrets of the advantages they have over other people. Indeed, it seemed they liked nothing better than to share them with other folk!

So, having observed what Christians do, and something more of what Christians are, I became increasingly keen to find out *how and why* they were different. So I began to attend church services myself, and it slowly dawned on me that it could only be GOD who was making those tremendous differences to their lives.

Then one evening a Christian school-teacher I had come to know quite well asked me these vital questions: *"Andrew, are you a Christian? Do you know what I am talking about?"*

Yes, by then I did know what she was talking about. For, slowly, and over those many years, as I have explained, I had come to recognize that the physical Universe contains a spiritual realm also. And I had come to recognise, through the differences between the lives of Christians and others, that God is real. Just as importantly I had long realised that, by myself, I could neither make my own life acceptable to God, nor significantly help others with theirs.

So I had to admit to my friend that, no, I was not a Christian.... but *I wanted to become one*! She then explained how I must pray to God - even though I had never really tried to speak to Him personally before; I must seek His forgiveness for neglecting Him, and breaking His laws; and invite Him to take control of my life in every way, and so give me the peace I had long desired.

I did all this, and the results in my life since then have been incredible! My only regret is that I was such a *slow learner* so far as God and the spiritual Universe are concerned!

Editor:    Andrew, thank you for these very personal things you have shared with us today. Permit me to add just one more point which occurs to me following your comments on both

Chemistry and Christianity: *no-one can learn from the knowledge and experience of someone else unless they really want to*! I am sure you have known many school students who have not wanted to learn Chemistry: and few if any of these have become the professional chemists of today. Similarly, many of our readers may not have been interested previously in learning about Christianity, and are therefore not professing Christians. But there is good news with which to conclude: whilst it may be too late for many of us to become professional chemists, there is *still the opportunity for those who have not yet become Christians to do so -* NOW!

# 12.

# WASHED ALL THROUGH

**Peter Schwemlein**
(*Nuclear Health Physicist, Barnwood, Gloucestershire, England*)

**Peter Schwemlein** *has spent most of his working life as a Nuclear Health Physicist, living today in western England. He is a member of the Editor's church in the city of Bristol. Peter's job has been to help prevent nuclear accidents of any scale from happening.... but also to lessen their impact should they do so. Having family roots in Central Europe as well as England, Peter has recently strengthened further his links with that region through active involvement with church growth projects in north-west Hungary.*

*The other two most important facets of Peter's personal life are much longer-established, namely his professional career, and his strong Christian faith. Leaving school in Bournemouth with Advanced Level General Certificate of Education examination passes in Mathematics and Physics, he then studied for his Higher National Certificate in Physics at the University of the West of England, before graduating as Master of Science in Radiation Protection from the University of Surrey. He now works with Nuclear Power, one of the two major electric power generation companies in the United Kingdom.*

*However, Peter considers that his* most important qualification *was gained at the tender age of 10: as he explains, this is when he was washed clean by God from all the sins in his life. Linking his long-*

*standing Christian experience and the work he does in his*
*professional career, Peter has come to see a number of parallels*
*between Nuclear Health Physics and the Christian faith, as he*
*discusses here with Dr. Barrett....*

---

Editor:    Peter, your surname 'Schwemlein' clearly is not English! Tell
           us first how you have come to have it.

Peter:     You're right. 'Schwemlein' is not an English, but an Austrian,
           name. My father came from German stock in Voyvadena, an
           area which is now in the Republic of Slovenia, not far from
           its border with Austria. After being taken prisoner of war by
           the Allies during World War II he came to England to work
           on a farm. A qualified chef, he was cooking a meal for a
           special event one day when he met the English girl he later
           married. They set up home in this country, and I am one of
           the results - an Englishman with a germanic name!

Editor:    That is an interesting family history! And I have reason to
           believe your work is interesting too. Your job title is 'Nuclear
           Health Physicist'; there cannot be too many of these in the
           United Kingdom!

Peter:     No, there are not. After all, there are only about a dozen
           nuclear power stations in the whole country. Unlike several
           other advanced industrialised countries I could name, we in
           the UK have not developed a high reliance on nuclear energy
           to meet our national power demands.

Editor:    Is this because we in Britain came to appreciate the potential
           dangers associated with nuclear power stations sooner than
           most others?

Peter:     No, I don't think so, although we were certainly among the
           first to consider such problems seriously, and in considerable
           detail. No, we built relatively few nuclear power stations
           because, when nuclear power was becoming popular, large oil
           and gas fields were being discovered in the British sector of
           the North Sea. The result is that only about 17% of our
           national power requirements are met by nuclear power
           stations - less than in many other countries. For example, in

Belgium the comparable figure is over 50%, and in neighbouring France it is over 70%!

Editor:  In recent years the whole world has become very conscious of some of the dangers associated with nuclear power stations. I can think of several power stations which have become household names because of major nuclear accidents - including Three Mile Island in Pennsylvania, USA, and Chernobyl in The Ukraine. Major nuclear power station accidents can have serious consequences for people over very wide areas. But such dangers are most threatening at a local level - as our national newspapers are quick to point out, whenever there is some leak of radiation into the environment, even if this leak is quite minor! I understand your job involves local, as well as wider, effects of nuclear power station accidents?

Peter:  Yes, it does. It is assumed that all radioactive material is detrimental to life, and that any radioactive contamination of the environment can be harmful to people, plants and animals. As you may know, even *natural* radioactivity - for example radon gas, which is given off by natural materials in the ground, such as granite rocks - can be harmful if its concentration is high enough. If people are exposed to radon over long periods of time the risks of exposure to these natural emissions can be very significant. In such cases we can't remove the radiation at its source, but we can usually provide satisfactory protection to people living in affected areas by simple modifications to their homes.

As far as radioactive leaks from *artificial* sources such as power stations are concerned, they are rarely large or concentrated, but the releases of radiation from major nuclear accidents can be absolutely devastating! Because these consequences can be so severe, enormous efforts are applied to the design and management of nuclear stations so that the risk of such events is very small indeed. It's my responsibility as a Nuclear Health Physicist to help ensure that this is so.

Editor:  Now we have got the general picture, tell us more specifically how safety is sought in and around nuclear power stations.

Peter:  Three things are particularly important.

First, careful design of each power station, to minimise the risk of nuclear plant failures which may lead to a release of radioactive material.

Second, careful control of power station operations, including provisions for rapid responses to any tendencies for a system to stray outside safe operating criteria.

And third, careful management of the work-force, and their working methods, not least for their own protection. Indeed, this is particularly important for maintenance engineers who have to work close to the reactors or their cooling systems, such as in the steam generators. For example, when uranium 235 undergoes fission it produces so-called 'daughter products' which deposit on the cooling system walls. The cooling systems must be inspected routinely to ensure that contaminated water does not leak into the secondary circuit. For every major repair job inside the reactor building, a safe working period has to be calculated for the maintenance engineers, involving the radiation dose rate they experience, the distance they must try to keep from the radiation source, and the degrees of shielding with which the engineers must be provided, all to prevent unacceptable levels of body contamination.

Editor:  And yet, despite all such precautions, we know that accidents sometimes happen, and radiation leaks occur! What is the role of the Nuclear Health Physicist then?

Peter:  The important thing in such circumstances is to confirm that the reactor itself - the source of the radiation - is under control, then to repair sources of any leaking radiation. The health physicist will be on hand to take measurements and advise where it is safe to work, and for how long.

Editor:  Let us suppose for a moment that I, as a visitor to a nuclear power station, became accidently exposed to a significant leak of radiation. What treatment would you give me?

Peter:  First of all you would be given decontamination treatment, to restrict as far as possible the damage to your body. Washing is always helpful, to remove external contamination on the skin. For serious inhalation exposures it is even possible to 'wash out' the lungs. If any radiation had been absorbed by your body tissues that would be much more difficult to remove. In this case we would probably have to wait for you to recover naturally!  In some caes, medication might help, but in very extreme situations, surgery might be necessary to remove badly damaged organs, for example to replace your bone marrow.  But I am afraid that, if you had been exposed to a large amount of radiation, perhaps as one of the workers trying to repair a damaged reactor, no treatment at all would be successful: you would die sooner, perhaps much sooner, than otherwise!

Editor:  Hmm, yes, it is clear that *prevention* is much better than *cure*!  And to make life even more difficult for the Nuclear Health Physicist, I guess it is not only the presently operating power stations themselves which may pose a threat, but old, decommissioned stations too?

Peter:  You are absolutely right!  Let me say a little about disposal of spent uranium rods from power stations, for this is a particularly difficult problem.  It is very important that humans do not come into contact with these, and that contamination from the rods does not enter the food chain.  Therefore, such waste is treated with great care.  After chemical treatment the waste is encased in ceramic material, embedded in steel and concrete, then buried in specially excavated caves deep in the ground!

I'd suggest it is a great pity we do not treat things that can contaminate our *souls* with at least as much caution!

Editor:  That is a very interesting suggestion, Peter!  But what suddenly made you think of that?

Peter:  Oh, it wasn't sudden!  Having been a Christian for many years I have long been interested in parallels between the physical and spiritual worlds.  And where better could I start thinking about these than in the realm of my own professional work?

Editor:  Where indeed!  Our work-places are very good places for all of us to search for insights into what life is all about!  But please, tell us how you became a Christian.  For no-one is *born* a Christian.  Indeed, there is obviously something in us which insists that we all naturally rebel against God, and reject His ways.

Peter:  There is indeed.... and I was certainly no exception to that!  But I wasn't very old before I learnt more sense.  Although my father did not go to church at all, my mother used to play the piano in the local church. So, as a compromise when I was a young lad, I went to church once every two weeks. I was not really helped by my church-going, though, until I was 10 years old. Then, one Sunday, the visiting preacher really got excited about what he had to say. He got so excited that I recall him removing his jacket so that he could make his points even more vigorously! I was so impressed by his earnestness that for the first time in my life I actually listened consciously to what he was saying. I can't tell you exactly now what this was, but I do remember it involved the Biblical insistence that one day all of us will be judged by God, for all we have done. I remember thinking that I could be in real trouble if I was to be judged by God just then! Of course, if we knew exactly when we would die and be judged by God, we would all get ready for it in time. Unfortunately, the Bible also makes it very clear that none of us can ever know when that will be. The chief result is that many people do not feel any sense of *urgency* about the need to be forgiven by God, even for breaking His commandments often.

Editor:  Did you seek God's forgiveness that same day?

Peter:  No, I didn't - but I thought about these things all the following week, and, next Sunday broke my usual pattern and went back to church again. For it had become clear to me that I needed to be saved from the consequences of all I'd done wrong. I recognized, too, that God's Son, Jesus Christ, had already suffered the death penalty so that everyone who trusted Him could go free - and that included me! All these thoughts affected me so deeply that at the end of the service that next Sunday I broke down and cried. I was upset because, although I was only a young lad, I knew that I was - in the language of the Bible - a sinner against God, and was not ready to meet God as judge. There and then friends helped me ask Him to forgive me for the past, and to claim that Jesus Christ had paid the penalty I myself had deserved.

I knew *at once* that my prayer had been answered, for the relief I felt then was enormous! There was much I didn't know or understand about God at the time - but those few basic things I've outlined were enough to begin to bring about great changes in my life and behaviour, especially at home, where my parents were most impressed!

Editor:   You said a little earlier that you have seen parallels between physical and spiritual truths in your place of work. Can you give us an example of something from your everyday work which can be an image of spiritual reality? You began by reminding us that nuclear power stations basically *benefit* us all because they are very valuable sources of energy - but *threaten* us all, because dangerous by-products result from nuclear fission. Is this a good starting point for a spiritual analogy?

Peter:    Yes, I think it is. You see, the Universe we live in is also a masterpiece of design - but there is evil at work in it which can be highly damaging to human beings. The Bible has much to say about this. For example, the Old Testament prophecy of Habakkuk lists *violence, injustice, wrongs, destruction, strife* and *conflict* as evil by-products of human society which affect everybody. If we embrace such things ourselves, we sin, both against God and our fellow men.

It is also clear from the Bible that God knew about the potential for evil in the world when He made mankind! And, as the old adage put it *"prevention is better than cure"*, so far as both radiation contamination, and what we may call 'sin-sickness', are concerned! Therefore, in the beginning God designed a 'safety envelope' for men and women to live in: so long as they obeyed Him fully they would enjoy life, and be free from pain and death. But most people know from the story of Adam and Eve in the Garden of Eden that men and women quickly began to ignore the Maker's instructions! So God, in the imagery of the Biblical book of Genesis, had no choice but to banish people from that place where life had previously been entirely enjoyable, and safe.

Thus, in their own way the results of sin have been every bit as bad as strong overdoses of harmful radiation.... indeed even more so, for the effects of sin often harm not only the body, but also the *soul*.... resulting not only in the death of the body, but death of the spirit too - painful separation from God! Living apart from Him is REALLY hazardous! And, you should understand, the effects of evil upon our souls are really very similar to those of radioactivity upon our bodies:

in both cases the greater the exposure, the more obvious and rapid the results!

Editor:    You told us earlier that there are treatments which can often help people who have been exposed to radioactive contamination. Can these treatments help us understand how people like you and me can be cured from the results of exposure to sin?

Peter:     Yes, they can! First there must be a process of *spiritual decontamination*!   You'll remember that radioactive contamination can often be removed from its victim by washing. The Bible, speaking metaphorically, says that we can be cleansed - completely! - by the blood of Jesus. The effect of this is that God will consider us to be completely free from sin if we claim that He paid the death penalty instead of us, and thank God for His sacrifice on our behalf. This 'washing away' of sin is not only *external*, causing immediate changes in our behaviour, but is also *internal* - amounting to complete inner cleansing, cleansing of our entire personalities! It's so complete that the Bible describes this as being *"washed all through"*.

Editor:    Earlier you spoke also of the need for more serious medical treatment, such as replacing bone marrow, if radioactive contamination has been severe. Is there any spiritual analogy here too?

Peter:     I think there is.  In many cases people will find that, on becoming Christians, there are attitudes, thought patterns, and related activities which are unacceptable to God: they must be replaced if we are to please God in everything. To quote the Bible again, we become *"new creatures"* when God enters our lives.

But a word of caution is in order!  It is also true that, as radiation can cause permanent damage to our bodies, the results of exposure to sin can leave us with lasting problems of its own, for sin etches its effects onto our bodies, our minds, and our souls. It is true that God forgives us if we ask Him to, and thereafter cares for us as if we had never sinned at all; but He does not usually remove from us all the consequences of things we previously did wrong! And this is a very good reason for seeking His help very early in life, as I was able to do. The later we delay this, the worse the effects that sin can have on us.

Editor: You have explained how God originally designed a way for people to live so that evil should not damage us spiritually.... and how He is able to remove its worst effects from our lives if we ask Him to. Perhaps we can extend this analogy, or set of analogies, one stage further. I guess that, just as your colleagues can work in potentially hazardous parts of power stations most safely by observing certain codes of conduct, so it must be possible for us, once we have been spiritually cleansed, to avoid harmful influences of sin in the world around us by following appropriate sets of spiritual rules?

Peter: Exactly! And the Biblical New Testament neatly compresses these rules into just two: *love God with all the strength we have....* and *love other people as much as we love ourselves*!

Editor: Simple commands indeed - but impossible even to attempt without the help of God Himself!

Peter, thank you very much for sharing all these thoughts. I hope that others will think through these issues - and act accordingly. Unlike you, most of us cannot exercise any control over *radiation* in our physical environments.... but we can all take steps to lessen the effects of *sin*, both around us and within us. The job you do is clearly a vital one, but the benefits of the thoughts you have shared could be much longer lasting - and will be, if people act on them, individually, as you yourself have done. The key thing is for them to ask God to *cleanse them from all sin*, and then *protect them from all spiritual evil* in the world!

# 13.

# RICHES WORTH HAVING

**Teresita Natividad**
*(Mathematician, International Fund for Agricultural Development, Rome, Italy)*

*Environmental Remote Sensing is a new Science with many applications to the Less Developed Countries of the world. Thus, the Editor - a pioneer in the use of satellites for environmental monitoring - has worked on many occasions with the Food and Agriculture Organisation (FAO) Agency of the United Nations, frequently visiting its International Headquarters in Rome, Italy. Rome contains offices of many international organisations, as a result of which some of its churches hold English-language services, and are attended by Christians from many different countries.*

*   **Teresita Natividad** is a native of the south-east Asian island nation of The Philippines. Born and brought up in its capital, Manila, she is a Mathematics graduate of the University of the Philippines in that city. More recently she has been employed by the International Fund for Agricultural Development (IFAD) in Rome.*

*   Dr. Barrett first met Teresita in English-speaking Rome Baptist Church.... and was immediately impressed by the unusual intensity of her desire to help improve living conditions and standards in the more deprived countries of the world, a desire which her professional work with IFAD was helping to satisfy. He learnt that the source of Teresita's concern for poor people lay in her own home*

*environment in the The Philippines where her own family had been*
*very poor, and where she had found herself teaching children who*
*were shoeless, dressed in ragged clothes, and even sometimes without*
*enough to eat.*

*But Teresita's concern for such folk is strongest because she herself*
*has come to realise, through particularly troubled times in her own*
*life, that* material wealth *is much less to be desired than* spiritual
riches. *These riches are the free gift of God to all who put their faith*
*in Him, whatever money or possessions they might or might not own.*
*Teresita's personal vision is not just to help the underprivileged of the*
*world to improve their living standards, but much more to share with*
*others those riches which are not exhausted, but multiplied, as they*
*are shared with others.*

*This is her story, as told to the Editor in Rome.*

———   ———

Today, I work for the International Fund for Agricultural
Development. Not surprisingly we call it 'IFAD' for short! This is not
a *budget*, as the name seems to imply, but an *agency*, an agency of the
United Nations which seeks to promote improvements in agriculture in
the Developing Countries of the world. In my section we're concerned
with the management of loans to small farmers. I can well understand
the needs of such people, for many of them are very poor, and I come
from a very poor background myself.

You may wonder how a girl from a very poor family in The
Philippines could come to work for the United Nations in Rome. Well,
a good education has helped enormously!

There were several things that made my good education possible.
One was that I nearly always did well in my examinations. In
elementary school I got many medals and honours for my work. When
14 years old I sat the examination to be graded in my secondary
school. I did so well in that exam that I was put in the highest grade.
Later, I had the chance to go to a very select school - Quezon City
Science High School in Manila. This is one of the best schools in the
whole of The Philippines. Because I did well academically, no fees
were charged for me to attend it. Then I won a place at the National
University, to study Mathematics. Because my family was so poor,

an Aunt gave me some money to pay for my dormitory bed, and for food.

Now the main reason why my own family was so poor was because my father left us when I was very small. My mother, my two brothers and I went to live with my grandmother. Without a man's income, life was very difficult. My brothers both worked after school each day to pay some of the bills and continue their education. One worked as a building labourer - the other as a comic artist! But I resented our poverty. I became so troubled by it that I really suffered psychologically. I just couldn't accept that we should have so little materially while some other people, like those in the wealthier suburbs of Manila, had so much. Because our poverty embarrassed me, I had few friends. I began to reason when I was in my early teens that the only way out of poverty, to the life-style I coveted, was through education. So when I went to the Science High School I would sometimes sit up all night working at my Mathematics so that I would excel at it. As direct consequences of what had happened to our family, I had other psychological problems too. One was a deep mistrust of men! I don't remember even seeing my father until I was 15 years old. People said *"Your father left you all: he is bad!"* So I blamed him for our situation, and thought all men were similarly irresponsible.

Things did not improve when I first went to university. Indeed, at first they got worse - much worse! My personal and emotional problems increased. I discovered that most of my student colleagues had complete families at home.... and were well provided for. To cover my embarrassment, and to try to forget my problems, I began to drink alcohol heavily. I became a chain smoker too. Instead of studying, I began to spend whole nights at discos, and 'folk houses' where people drank beer, and sang bawdy songs. I even carried a knife with me, and threatened, or fought, men with it. Not surprisingly no-one liked me! I was a social misfit. And for the first time in my life I began failing my exams. I realised that I might not be able to look to my education any more to pull me up out of all my problems. I should have blamed myself for this situation, but blamed others more and more instead. I blamed my *father* all the more for leaving us. I blamed my *family* for not earning more. I even blamed *God* for my unacceptable behaviour: in His case, I reasoned to myself that if He really cared for people, my own situation would surely be much better!

That was, of course, an unfair indictment of God, but I did not know very much about Him at that time. I did believe there was a God. I didn't find that difficult, even as a Science student. I knew many people worshipped Him and prayed to Him. Indeed, I myself had tried praying to Him many times, especially when I was younger. But I never seemed to get through to Him at all. So, as I grew older, I grew to accuse Him for my problems, more and more.... and my life went from bad to worse. But, when I had begun my final year of study, something very unexpected happened: to me it seemed like a real miracle! Certainly it brought about a great change in my life. And God was very much involved in this: I am sure I could never have brought about such a change myself!

One of the girls I met at university was a Christian. I knew that she set aside one day each week specifically to go to church, and to work for the church.

*"Why do you do this?"* I asked.

*"Because the Bible says 'Remember the Sabbath day by keeping it holy'"*, she replied, quoting Exodus, Chapter 20, Verse 8. I thought it stupid that anyone should take any notice of the Bible. But, little by little, I began to wonder if it could be relevant to life at the end of the Twentieth Century.

Then, one day, I went to a radio studio to see someone I knew there, a girl disc jockey. I found her talking to another Christian - an evangelical, I believe. We three chatted to each other as the records played, between each announcement. One thing the Christian was explaining was that, although she liked a certain man, she could not live with him, and could not marry him, because he was not a Christian Believer too.

*"How stupid!"* I remarked. *"Why bother about what the Bible says?"* And I tried to argue that much of the Bible could be disproved, and the rest of it did not make sense.

We argued about this for a while. Then suddenly the Christian girl asked me a direct question! *"Terisita,"* she said, *"You haven't asked God to save you from the consequences of your sins, have you?"*

I fumbled for an answer.

Then, recalling those times I'd tried to tell God my grievance about my poverty, I blurted out triumphantly, *"Yes I have! I have asked Him to save me!"*

There was a brief silence.

*"BUT"* said the girl quietly, *"God has made this promise to His people: 'I will never leave you, nor forsake you.' Once He has saved you, you are ALWAYS saved....!"*

I understood immediately what she was saying! She had seen through my deceit, and had confronted me with it: I had not asked God to save me from the consequences of my *sins* - but from my POVERTY! I realised that most of my plight was of my own making! My father was somewhat to blame, but through my own attitudes and actions I had made matters worse. And instead of apologising to God for all I had done wrong myself, I had wrongly accused HIM of causing me to do it.

My new friend continued: *"I don't believe you have ever asked Him to forgive you for your own wrongs"*, she concluded. *"Why don't you do so now"?*

I was really on the spot! I nodded dumbly, for once completely speechless. She prayed with me, and I pretended I had really made my peace with God. That way I pleased her, and managed to escape discussing the subject further. But I still wasn't at peace, either with God, or with myself.

That night, I couldn't sleep at all.

I was battling with myself, particularly with my pride. I could see now that most of my problems had not been caused by other people. For most of them I could really only blame myself.

All next day too I was torn by inner conflict.

Then, in the evening, I couldn't struggle any more! I locked my door. I knelt down by my bed and wept. I recalled the prayer of penitence and commitment to God that my friend had prayed for me in the radio studio, and repeated it myself. A *split second* later I knew that God was present with me, and that He had responded to my prayer! My tears of grief changed to tears of relief and joy. The vicious circle had been broken. With God's help, I could begin to build a new and better life.

Of course, this was not achieved all at once. I still found it hard to be humble before God. But my knowledge and understanding of Him began to grow, and I'm sure I began to become a much better person as a result. One of the first things I had to do after I became a Christian was to go and apologise to the guys I'd terrorised with my knife. That probably shook them more than any of my earlier attacks on them had done! Then I read in the Bible that *"your body is a temple of the Holy*

*Spirit"* (Paul's First Letter to the Corinthians, Chapter 6, Verse 19). As I thought about this, I began to lose the taste for alcohol and cigarettes, both of which had been injuring my health. This brought other benefits too: I was able to use much more responsibly the little money I had at my disposal!

Then I decided I ought to depend on God to provide for me each day, rather than on my aunt, for she herself could scarcely afford to help me. Wonderfully, God led me to a Christian hostel where my bed was provided free of charge. And my room-mate gave me food all through that last year of my degree course. Earlier, no-one would ever have done that: remember, people used to hate me! But now I was beginning to witness and experience the love Christians have for other people because they themselves have benefited from the love of God.

So I began to study more effectively again, and passed my Final Examinations for the degree of Bachelor of Science, with Honours, though only two or three of us out of an original class of 20 or so in my college did so. There was one thing, though, that I almost lived to regret: a bargain I had struck with God! I know now that it's not wise to bargain with Him - and *very presumptuous* for any of us to do so! But at one point I had said this to Him: *"Lord, allow me to graduate - and you can use me wherever you like!"*

After graduation, where did He send me first?

To teach Mathematics in a High School in a slum area, in one of the poorest parts of Manila! ME - who had so hated being poor! But, you know, in that area I began to see that when I had been in similar circumstances I myself had had privileges, but had never recognised them as such: in my school, many of the kids were so poor that they came to school each day without proper clothing, and with no shoes on their feet!

But as I thought about my bargain with God, I began to realize that He must have had His own purposes for sending me to such an area. This gave me courage to witness to my pupils, concerning the love God has for everyone, and which He will give them if they will let Him help them in their personal lives. These pupils ranged from 16 - 25 years old. And then another miracle happened! Within a couple of days threequarters of them accepted Jesus Christ as their own, personal Saviour! It was amazing! Many came to me weeping, and asking forgiveness from God for the wrong things they'd done. God's spirit swept through that school: when He moves, He can be

IRRESISTIBLE!

Soon, with the help of other Christians on the staff, Bible study groups were set up. Then, although I was still only in my twenties, I was appointed Principal of that school! The Administrator allowed me to include Bible Study as part of the normal curriculum. I left recently, but the Bible Study groups are still meeting - and growing. This was in an area where there had been no local church, and because the people are too poor to afford bus fares to churches elsewhere, very few were Christians. But now a new church has been established, called the 'Balra Christian Fellowship', and this is meeting many needs in that community.

In view of such exciting developments I often ask myself why God has brought me to Rome, to a very different kind of occupation. But I believe this, too, is for His purposes. One day the full reasons will become plain. If we trust God, He guides us in all our ways! In Balra I began to sense He wanted me somewhere else. One day I read Paul's message in the Bible, in his Second Letter to Timothy, Chapter 4, part of whose theme is *"My work here is finished"*. That spoke to my heart. I felt God was leading me here to Rome, even though I did not have a job to come to. But I soon found employment with IFAD, and as I said earlier, my own background of poverty gives me special understanding of the importance of the IFAD programme for poor rural communities. It is already giving me great satisfaction to think I can help such people in some small way.

My future, though, is entirely in God's hands. Remember, He helped me get my degree.... and I promised Him that He could then use me wherever He chose....!

# 14.

## MENDING A MARRIAGE

**Dr. Dane Clark**
(*Division Manager, NOAA Satellite Services, Washington DC, USA*)

and
**Jenifer Clark**
(*Oceanographer, NOAA, Washington DC, USA*)

*Life should be great: you're a top scientist in a government laboratory, undertaking internationally important work with practical benefits for many.*

*But your private life is beset by problems: your marriage ends in divorce; you engage in affairs with a number of other people; you become depressed. Whose help should you seek?*

*This set of experiences, and this related question, confronted not just* one *person known professionally by the Editor, but* TWO. *The lives of these two persons have since converged, and their personal experiences have continued to be so amazingly similar that this Chapter includes them both.*

**Dr. Dane** *and Jenifer Clark work in the US National Oceanic and Atmospheric Administration (NOAA) Science Center on the outskirts of Washington DC, the US capital city. Dane holds degrees in Science, Meteorology, and Business, and serves the NOAA Satellite Service as a Divison Level Manager Meteorologist. His wife, Jenifer, has degrees in Mathematics and Oceanography, and is an*

*Oceanographer with NOAA, working in the same building as Dane.*

*Both Dane and Jenifer confess to having critical, analytical minds. And, in the midst of their similar personal and family problems, they both arrived - though in quite different ways - at the same answers to their most urgent questions. In this Chapter, the transcript of a recent discussion with Dr. Barrett in Washington DC, both Dane and Jenifer share these answers with us, and how they reached them. They tell us, too, how their marriage was mended as God renewed their lives.... and how, in a most amazing way, He has now blessed their marriage with a child.*

---

Editor:   Dane, your Personal History form tells me you have earned three academic degrees.... you are a Division Manager in this office.... and your employer has honoured you with several 'Outstanding Achievements Awards'. This is quite a record! Give us some more details about yourself, and your work today.

Dane:   My first two degrees, a Bachelor of Science and a Master of Science, were both in Meteorology. I got them from Florida State University. My other degree is in a different area of study. It's a Master's Degree in Business Administration. But I guess this one is just as valuable to me in my present role as a NOAA Manager! The task of my Division is to produce a wide range of operational satellite weather products - including charts, diagrams, and maps - and to provide supports for national and international weather services. As you know the NOAA Science Center is housed in the World Weather Building, because of our function as one of the three main hubs of the World Weather Watch - the central programme which the World Meteorological Organization coordinates to make global weather forecasting possible. The two other hubs are in Moscow, Russia, and Melbourne, Australia.

Editor:   Tell us more about your Outstanding Achievements Awards.

Dane:   I guess there's not much more to say about them! They just say that my employer has specially appreciated my work.

Editor:   I am sure that is a much too modest view - but we will not embarrass you by pressing you further on this point! Would you say, though, that you have been successful in *everything* you have done?

Dane:     Oh no, I certainly would not! Indeed, until 1980 my personal life was largely unsuccessful! For one thing, I began drinking alcohol heavily, and taking drugs. Then I really made a mess of my first marriage. Things got so bad that divorce seemed the only way out of some of my problems. So I left my wife, and we became divorced. Those were really tough times. I became so depressed I sought help from a psychotherapist. That's not exactly a picture of a successful guy, is it!

Editor:   No, it is not! But it is clear you are not suffering from depression now. What caused the big turnaround?

Dane:     My cure wasn't any thing, it was a *person*! And that person certainly wasn't me: I was in no position to help myself at all.
          By then I had married for a second time. But my cure wasn't my second wife, Jenifer, either. She had many problems similar to my own. Not surprisingly, the early part of our marriage to each other had rough and stormy times!
          And it wasn't the psychotherapist who turned my life around. I stopped seeing him in the middle of 1980: by then our roles had reversed, and I had begun trying to help him with his own personal needs instead!
          The person who turned me around was - GOD!

Editor:   It is obvious, both from your work in Meteorology, and your administrative position, that you have a good analytical mind. Did that help, or hinder, your search for Him?

Dane:     Oh, I'm sure it helped, although in the end it was more a case of God finding me, than me finding Him. I had learned a good deal about God before then, for I had often gone to church when I was a teenager, even though my parents were not Christians. But I had missed some vital points!
          So, grown up, and with my personal life disintegrating, I should have feared God because I had so neglected and disobeyed Him. But the thing I feared most was death. I began to explore the mystical world, the world of the psychic: I tried to find hope for my future in the spirit world. I discovered that many people claim paranormal abilities. One

of my new acquaintances could go into trances, and tell a group of us things about other people - things we didn't see how he could know without supernatural help.

But much of what I read of people claiming supernatural powers seemed selfish and evil. I analyzed their explanations of the world, and human life and society. And most of them lacked credibility. That's one reason I became so depressed! Then my first marriage broke up, and I was really in a bad way personally. I couldn't see a ray of hope anywhere.

Editor:    You said just now that your life changed after you met God. But not so much because *you* found God - but because *He* found you! How did you begin to realize that He is real, and became aware that He cared for you?

Dane:    Oh, there were many ways. Let me tell you two that I remember vividly.

One of the first was when I was watching a TV drama. I became aware that everything it showed involved a struggle: a struggle between good and evil. Suddenly I realized that good and evil forces were battling in my life too. I sensed that my life was on a precipice. That really shook me up, I can tell you! I concluded that this awareness must have come from someone good - who wanted to rescue me from grave danger.

So, I became conscious of a spiritual presence impressing me that I was loved and cared for, even in the smallest details of my life. Gradually I became sure it was God who was speaking to me, and that, if He was so good and powerful, I should listen to what He had to say.

Editor:    The big change in your life came soon after that? Tell us how it took place.

Dane:    There's a programme on television in this country called the 'PTL Club'.

Editor:    The 'PTL Club'? You will have to interpret that!

Dane:    It is the 'Praise The Lord Club'! This is a Christian programme about things God does for people. Many of these are so remarkable they just make us praise Him for being so good.

This wasn't a programme I was in the habit of watching - far from it! But I happened to hear that the subject one evening was going to be *"The Truth about Mysticism."* Being analytical, truth appeals to me. Having been so involved in the mystical world, I was doubly interested. So I watched the programme. Right from the start my attention was rivetted. The speaker began this way: *"If you're into mysticism,"* he said *"stay tuned! I've been into it too, all the way. It didn't help me! And there's nothing in it for you, either!"*

I couldn't disagree with that: that had been exactly my own experience! I went on watching. The presenter stressed that there is one and only one spiritual Being who cares for us, and can positively help us, in this life or the next. That one is God. He's the One who not only gives us hope of better things, but also gives us His Son, Jesus Christ, so that that hope can be fulfilled. This seemed to confirm my own recent experiences too. Logically, all the speaker claimed could be correct. Suddenly it struck me that analysis alone could not take me any further! In that instant I was *absolutely sure* this man was speaking the truth.... but it would make no difference to me *unless I acted on it*!

Then and there I surrendered myself to God. I asked His forgiveness for all the things I had done that had caused the mess I was in. And I asked Him to help me rebuild my life in a new a better way.

Only a day or two after that submission of my will to Him, a consciousness of the total change this had brought about in my life suddenly hit me. *"WOW!"* I thought. *"What IS this?! It's so GREAT! If only I'd known of it before! Think of the heartaches which would have been avoided!"*

Editor:   That is when you stopped seeing the psychiatrist?

Dane:    Yes, or shortly after. He had helped me somewhat, but it was God who made the difference I really needed. And God made the same difference to my new wife, soon afterwards.

From time to time Jenifer and I encounter new problems in our lives, but we're not worried, because we know God helps us overcome them. Life's great now. God is so good to us. We've seen Him bring about such tremendous changes in our lives, and the lives of others! And, in quite an astonishing way He has blessed our marriage to each other with little Rachel. She is the child we so much wanted; we had prayed for her for over eight years, but had been unable to conceive.

Editor: Rachel's story is certainly astonishing! I have seen the banner headline in *"The Journal"*, the daily newspaper from the area where you live, Prince George's County in the State of Maryland. The headline proclaimed in big, bold type "INFANT FOUND IN TRASH BIN"! This abandoned baby became yours, by adoption?

Dane: Yes, she did: wasn't that amazing? Police said that this tiny child was only hours old when she was found in a sealed garbage bag in a dump site behind a flower shop! This discovery really hit the news headlines, in the papers, on radio, and TV too. Thousands of people wanted to adopt this beautiful baby girl, whose life God had wonderfully spared. Imagine our joy when she was entrusted to *us*! For this has been a very special fulfilment of the promise in Psalm 37: Verse 4, *"Delight yourself in the Lord, and He will give you the desires of your heart."* We have been wonderfully blessed by Him!

Editor: Thank you for being so open and honest, Dane. But now it is time we heard from your wife, Jenifer.

\*                    \*                    \*                    \*

Editor: Jenifer, hi! We have just heard a great story of God's grace from your husband. I am interested to learn more of the *similarities* between your experience and his. Dane began by telling us a little about his training, and his present work. Maybe this is a good place for you to begin, too!

Jenifer: Yes, I think it is. But first I'll tell you about some *dissimilarities* between his story and mine! One major difference involves my area of science: I'm not a Meteorologist! My Bachelor of Science degree was in Mathematics. Then I studied Oceanography, in Graduate School at Johns Hopkins University in Baltimore. So, although I now work next door to Dane in the World Weather Building, my field is not Meteorology, but Oceanography.

I am using some of the same data, though. In Dane's branch of NOAA, data from our environmental satellites are used to monitor the atmosphere. In mine, we look *through* the atmosphere, between the clouds, so we can monitor the surfaces of oceans and seas.

Editor:    What kinds of products do you prepare from the satellite data?

Jenifer:    Well, for one thing we produce daily charts of the major warm ocean current in the North Atlantic, the Gulf Stream. These charts are mainly for use by the fishing industry, and mariners. Then there is this monthly report which I write and edit, the *"Oceanographic Monthly Summary"*, published by the US Department of Commerce.

Editor:    Yes, I have seen a recent copy. It covered a wide range of topics.... Pacific and Atlantic sea surface temperatures, Bering Sea and North Slope ice.... Ocean Features of the East and West Coasts of North America.... and other things also. There is no doubt that your work is clearly different from Dane's!

But in other ways your story is very similar to his! For example, I believe you have been awarded for high quality work performance, as he has been!

Jenifer:    Well, yes, it's true, I have! One of my honour awards was cash, for a beneficial suggestion on how to make an ocean temperature data survey form more efficient by using computer techniques. Another was an 'Outstanding' rating for generally good work.

Editor:    Congratulations, Jenifer! But tell us about your personal life, and beliefs. These have not always been so meritorious, have they! We have heard how Dane went through a very rough patch in his life before he found God. How about you?

Jenifer:    In many ways our experiences in this area have been amazingly alike! For one thing I, too, was afraid of dying. For another thing, like Dane, I lost my way in my first marriage. I guess I was more dissatisfied with myself than with my first husband, but my first marriage also ended in divorce. At that time, as Dane had done, I sought help from a psychiatrist. We both had affairs with other people. Also like Dane, I had a little girl from my first marriage.

And at that time I didn't believe in God, or the Bible. So I was like him in that as well. To be truthful, my life was in a dreadful mess! Things improved somewhat when I met

Dane. We had had so many experiences in common, each of us could understand how the other felt. So we got married, and I was so glad my daughter Kim could have a father at home.

But things didn't get dramatically better until Dane became a Christian. Then I could see such a change in him, that I began to want to share this new thing he'd found. But I tried not to listen when Dane talked to me about God!

Editor: Tell us then, how did you come to find God yourself?

Jenifer: Things began to move towards a climax one night when Kim began crying and screaming. I ran up to her room.

*"Mummy,"* she said, *"I don't want to die! What happens then?"*

I couldn't give her a satisfactory answer: the same question had bothered me for years! I quietened her somehow. But then I saw a film about two boys. One had recently lost his father. The other was puzzled. *"How can you be so happy even though your father has just died?"* he asked. The boy's answer shook me. *"Because I'm a Christian"* he said. *"I know I will see him again, in heaven!"*

That was a kind of certainty I just didn't have!

Then Kim came back into the act again, but in a way which bothered me even more. She knew I was older than Dane. At that time I was only in my early 30s, but she was concerned for me. *"Tell me, what will happen when YOU die, Mummy?"* she implored. I gave a general answer in the form I knew she wanted, but without any personal conviction: *"If you believe in God, and belong to Him, you go to heaven"* I replied.

Kim thought about this.

A little later she asked the question which really put me on the spot: *"Mummy"*, she asked, *"do YOU believe in God?"*

I guess I had to be honest at last.

*"No"*, I said, *"I don't know HOW to believe in Him!"*

But Kim knew!

Sometimes we scientists can miss things that are so simple that even a child can see them: *"Mummy, you just have to have faith!"* was what she said....

Now Kim can be persistent when she likes! So the very next

day she asked me the same kind of question once more. *"Mummy, are you going to heaven?"* Guess what I said? *"YES, Kim! Because I believe in God!"*

And, do you know, this was true! The same moment I confessed God's existence, He gave me the power to believe in Him! Suddenly I was sure that God is real! And I realized He loved me, despite all my murky past. It's amazing how much He is prepared to forgive and forget.

Editor: This is a great testimony, Jenifer. But there is one thing I do not understand. It is hard to exercise simple faith in God if our minds are full of reasons why we think He cannot exist! What had happened to your earlier anti-God, anti-Bible, mindset?

Jenifer: Oh, God had already cleared my brain of that! You've heard of Josh McDowell, of 'Campus Crusade for Christ'?

Editor: Yes. He has written some excellent books which authenticate the Bible from credible non-Christian sources. *"Evidence that Demands a Verdict"* is one of the best of his books. It has been translated into many different languages.

Jenifer: That's right! Well, about the time of my discussions with Kim, I had been to one of Josh McDowell's conferences. In some ways it had been *shattering*! He had presented convincing arguments that all those things I had thought of as outrageously unbelievable in the Bible must be.... TRUE! I had learnt that even the astonishing claim that Jesus Christ rose from the dead has strong confirming evidence in the writings of respected historians.

So God had cleared my mind of false arguments, before He challenged me through Kim's questions. Like Dane, I'm a critical kind of person. My science training alone ensured that. But God had shown me, through Josh McDowell, that He had credibility.... and that what the Bible says is true.

After that, all I had to do was follow Kim's advice, and act on that discovery, by trusting God for myself.

Since my Christian conversion I've come to liken my experience to many a graph I could construct as a scientist. It rose slowly from the lowest, most negative point in my life, until I told Kim I believed in God. That was the real inflexion point, when my life moved into the zone of the positive. Since then it's been up and up!

For example, relationships within our family quickly improved. There was more love, and patience, and understanding everywhere! I'm now much less hot-tempered than I used to be. It used to take days for me to get over a disagreement with Dane. Now I find I can let go of anger much more easily. God is so good, and we've learnt more of Him every day, as a family.

Maybe I can sum up our experiences like this. *First*, God is real, even if we ever doubt His existence. Doubting doesn't do away with God!

*Second*, we discovered that God can speak to us about Himself in many ways. He spoke to Dane through television. He speaks to others through radio or through books. He spoke to me through my daughter, Kim. Any one or more of these, or other ways, may be the ones He chooses to speak through to us as individuals. But be sure of this: He will never *force* any of us to believe in Him! To find Him, we must desire to believe in Him ourselves.

Here's a *third* point. If God wants us, and we want Him, none of our past thoughts or deeds will be held against us! I have learnt that if we earnestly seek the forgiveness of God, He will give us a new start in life - despite whatever we have previously thought or done, because His Son, Jesus Christ, has once for all paid the penalty for all our sin.

My *last* point is this. God will accept people right away, if they are prepared to surrender themselves to Him. Dane and I have done this, and we know it is something we will never regret.

# 15.

# LIGHT AT THE END OF THE TUNNEL

**Eileen Maturi**
*(Physical Oceanographer, Satellite Applications Laboratory, NOAA, Washington DC, USA)*

*Mental Depression is one of the greatest human plagues of the present age. At any point in time millions of people are gripped by it, a frightening darkness which can seem both endless and impenetrable.*

*One who has experienced this darkness, and come out of it, is* **Eileen Maturi,** *a Physical Oceanographer working in the Satellite Applications Laboratory (SAL) of the US National Oceanic and Atmospheric Administration (NOAA) in Camp Springs, Maryland, USA. In this Laboratory, with which the Editor's own Research Centre has been formally linked since 1983 by a 'Memorandum of Understanding' for joint research, satellite and conventional data are brought together from many different sources. In SAL research is undertaken into the meanings of these data, leading to the development of new types of data products, advisories and warnings for dissemination to the relevant user communities. For several years Eileen has played an important part in this, in relation to ocean surface analyses and products development. She has two degrees from the University of Virginia, and has travelled very widely in pursuit of her scientific researches.*

*But Eileen's own "greatest discovery" relates primarily to an entirely different realm - and has proved the key to her re-emergence into the*

*light from the end of a dark tunnel of deep personal depression. Dr.*
*Barrett has known Eileen personally for several years because of his*
*frequent professional visits to SAL. He has seen for himself the great*
*changes in her that have come about since she came to know God*
*personally.*

---

Editor:  Eileen, we have known each other over quite a long time, but
there is much about your personal history I myself shall be
interested to learn. But first, for the sake of others, please
sketch something of your present professional position.

Eileen:  I am an Oceanographer in the Satellite Applications
Laboratory of NOAA. At present I am mainly occupied on
three projects. One is very practically orientated - the aptly-
named 'Coastwatch Program'. Here I am helping to develop a
range of sea reports based on satellite data for sailors and
fishermen in the coastal waters of North America. For
example, ice charts in winter, and plankton concentration
maps in summer. The second project is more research
focussed, involving air/sea interactions. The third is in
education and training, to help ensure that the new marine
observation products are used as widely as possible.

Editor:  How did you qualify for your present position?

Eileen:  At university I studied for a Bachelor of Science degree in
Physics, then for a Master of Science degree in
Oceanography. After that I had various jobs in United States
government oceanographic institutions - first as a computer
programmer in the Office of Naval Research, then as a
surveyor with the Naval Oceanographic Office, and after that
as a support scientist in the US State Department, helping to
define policies for the use and protection of the world's
oceans.

Editor:  Where did this work take you?

Eileen:  Literally all around the world! Along the west coast of the
USA.... off Alaska, Hawaii and the Philippines in the Pacific
Ocean.... around the Azores and the Canary Islands in the
Atlantic Ocean.... and to parts of the Mediterranean Sea.

My work included mapping the sea floor by acoustic instruments.... charting ocean currents by measuring the sea surface temperature.... establishing the rate and direction of water movement.... and evaluating chemical characteristics of the water itself.

Editor: Were these studies all made from ships?

Eileen: Some were, but many were made from aircraft. I have spent many hours working equipment in aircraft like the turboprop-engined Lockheed Orion.

Editor: Did you enjoy those types of work?

Eileen: For their research values, yes; but in other ways, no! You see, I was usually the only girl on board ship and often felt lonely and defensive. Meanwhile, on the aircraft we often had to fly as low as 60 metres above the sea surface, so the air turbulence could be very bad indeed. At times like those it was only my belief in God that saw me through!

Editor: Your *belief in God* saw you through?

Eileen: Yes, for most of my life I had considered myself a Christian. Many of my relatives are priests or missionaries, so I grew up with strong religious influences around me.

When I was 13 or 14 years old I began associating with a bad group of kids in my neighbourhood. But I saw where life without God could lead. So I realised the need to try to obey God, and live my life to His standards. By the time I went to college I knew it was more important to seek God's friendship than that of the opposite sex.

The church I attended at that time was very liturgical and ritualistic. However, through its many symbols I became really impressed with the power, the majesty, the *awesomeness* of God!

Editor: Is this what you have meant when you have spoken to others about your *"most exciting discovery"*?

Eileen: No, although it is great to realise that it was God who brought into being all the beauty and variety in the world. *And* to know that God spiritually rewards those who worship Him.

In my case, though, you'll recall that I grew up surrounded by reminders of who God is, and so quite gradually grew to appreciate His majesty and powers. So, my most exciting discovery has been much more recent, and a lot more rapid.

Editor:     Please tell us about this.

Eileen:     In 1989 and 1990 I went through a period of deep depression.
            It is hard to describe this experience, but in many ways it was
            like going through a dark night of my soul - a long, black
            tunnel which seemed to have no end. Many times I would
            come home from work and cry and cry. I took medication - I
            had many sessions with psychiatrists and psychoanalysts. I
            knew many people were praying for me, but for a long time I
            could not escape from the darkness.

Editor:     Did you ever fear that you would not recover from this?

Eileen:     No, actually I did not! Even though my faith in God at that
            time was very incomplete, I always knew God would protect
            me, because He had always done so previously. So I believed
            my depression would leave me sometime, but I did not know
            when.

Editor:     Now you are as happy and out-going as anyone I know! Was
            your *"best discovery"* linked with the lifting of your
            depression?

Eileen:     Yes, it was. In order to come out of it I had to learn that we
            cannot lead successful lives in our own strength, but in the
            strength God gives to those who seek to OBEY Him.
            Previously I had believed in God, and had been glad to accept
            His care and protection. But I had not met Him as a *close
            personal friend*: I had not asked Him to take complete control
            of my life. Finally I gave my life, just as it was, over to God.
            It was then I found I could begin to rely on Him to build it
            into the shape He wanted, not the shape I myself had wanted
            it to take.

            Even that did not happen all at once. Gradually, though, I
            could look back and see my depression lifting. I hadn't been
            able to help myself recover, but now I knew God Himself was
            helping me. That was a wonderful, a truly exciting,
            realisation!

            And as I increasingly prayed to Him and read the Bible, I
            knew He was listening and speaking to me much more
            directly than I had ever known before. Perhaps most
            remarkably of all, I found not only my knowledge, but much
            more importantly, my understanding of my Christian faith
            suddenly deepening, becoming much fuller and more

complete. It was as if my memory banks, which had been filled earlier with facts about God, now became alive, and much more meaningful because I now knew Him, personally. I am now able to worship Him much more freely and spontaneously, for He is not only the Creator of the Universe, but also a friend I appreciate.

I have now moved to a much less ritualistic church. Its simpler form of worship suits the freedom I now feel in my soul. But I thank God for the years I spent in more liturgical churches, because the symbols in their worship taught me much about God, things I now appreciate truly because I now know Him so much better.

Editor:   Eileen, thank you so much for sharing these very personal thoughts with us today. Clearly some of your quite recent experiences have been difficult, even painful for you, but it will be a real encouragement to many that there can be happy endings, even to life's darkest tunnels.

There are certainly some important messages which spring from your story.

One thing that occurs to me is that there are many things in the world today which, at the time, seem to promise hope for the future - but rarely deliver peace of mind or true personal happiness. Things which include career advancement, the extension of scientific knowledge, modern medicine and psychiatry, and even rich religious rituals.

Next, it is clear that complete commitment to God does not promise immunity from the pressures of modern life, and their worst effects - but such commitments *can* deliver release and recovery from even those problems which make us feel most helpless.

Last, but not least, the changes God brings about in people committed fully to Him must be clear and evident to others, and this is great, for these are types of blessings which richly deserve to be shared.

Eileen, YOUR *"best discovery"* can be that of others too! Hearts, minds and souls can be renewed and refreshed through unreserved faith in Jesus Christ. You are a shining witness to the truth of this: let us hope others, through reading this will become witnesses to it also.

# 16.

# STRENGTHENED BY STORMS

**Trevor Guymer**
(*Head, James Rennell Division for Ocean Circulation, Southampton Oceanography Centre, England*)

*The 'James Rennell Division' is located - appropriately - in the new Oceanography Centre in Southampton, England. Appropriately because in recent centuries Southampton has been one of the major seaports of this sea-faring nation, indeed of the world, and because the Oceanography Centre is the biggest grouping of oceanographic research institutes in the United Kingdom. The James Rennell Division is one of several groups at the Centre, and is funded by the UK's Natural Environment Research Council. Two departments of the University of Southampton are located in the Centre also, giving a total of about 500 staff plus several hundred students.*

**Trevor Guymer**, *who holds Bachelor and Master of Science degrees from Imperial College in the University of London, has recently assumed the leadership of the James Rennell Division, and is a leading international authority both on observing the oceans from space, and on patterns and processes of air/sea interface exchanges. His studies involve not only purely oceanic, but also many atmospheric, phenomena. Trevor Guymer's work has earned him the status of Fellow of the Royal Meteorological Society, and he has been accorded this Society's 'L.F. Richardson Prize' for some of his published research, on "The Nocturnal Jet", an ephemeral stream of* *fast-moving air which develops in the lower layers of the atmosphere in some regions of the world under calm, clear sky conditions.*

*Quite over-modestly, Trevor says that combining research interests in the air and the oceans is not such an intellectual feat as it may seem at first, because both air and water obey the same physical laws, those of Hydrodynamics. However, recognising parallels between physical, and spiritual, laws of the Universe clearly calls for considerable breadths and depths of knowledge and understanding, plus great flexibility of thought! In the following conversation with the Editor, recorded at a recent conference at the Royal Society in London, at which they were both speakers, Trevor shows that he has acquired a masterly knowledge of both physical and spiritual laws, and enjoys finding analogues of the spiritual realm within the physical realms of air and water.*

Editor:  Trevor, thank you for agreeing to tell us something not only about your work, but also about yourself. Give us some of that more personal background information first.

Trevor:  Perhaps I should begin with my education. My first degree was in Physics, from the University of Surrey. But I was really more keen to study Meteorology - one type of *applied* Physics - because of the interest I have had in the atmosphere since I was a child. Almost from the time I was a baby in a pram I enjoyed watching the clouds! And my Dad, who had been a navigator in the Royal Air Force, had had a practical interest in the weather, and this helped to encourage my own interest in it too. So, after graduating as Bachelor of Science in Physics, I was pleased to be able to study for a Master of Science degree in Meteorology from Imperial College, one of the colleges of the University of London.

I was then given the chance to work as a Research Assistant on the JASIN Project. This was the 'Joint Air/Sea Interaction' Project which involved participants from several European countries, plus the USA and Australia. No fewer than 14 ships and three aircraft took part in it.. Its primary purpose was to investigate, in greater detail than before, important patterns and processes which are found at the boundary, or 'interface', between the Earth's atmosphere and its oceans.

One significance of this boundary is that important exchanges take place across it. For example, heat can be transferred from the air to the water, or from the water to the air. Moisture can be transferred across that boundary too. These and other transfers play major parts in the shaping of the world's pattern of climates.

During my work on JASIN, I worked at IOS, the British Institute of Oceanographic Sciences (the forerunner of the Southampton Oceanography Centre). I found work there so fulfilling that I was really pleased when I was subsequently offered a permanent post in IOS!

Today, although much of my work still involves the atmosphere, my interest in the oceans is at least as great.

Editor:   I was specially interested in what you were saying about air/sea exchanges! It is easy to see that the oceans must be the main source of the moisture which gives rise to clouds.... and are therefore, indirectly at least, the main sources of most of the world's rainfall. I am aware, too, that great quantities of heat must be stored in the oceans. But what, I wonder, is the biggest effect of the oceans on global climates?

Trevor:   The biggest effect of the oceans, because of their enormous capacity to store heat, is to provide the *long-term memory* of the climate system. If we want to understand changes in climate over tens or hundreds of years, we need to know what's happening in the deep ocean. The fact that the temperature of the ocean changes only very slowly means that it acts as a moderating influence on the air above. A related fact is that, if there were no heat exchanges across the air/sea interface, all those land areas influenced by winds off the sea would have more extreme climates than they have today.

Editor:   And, since most people live on continents, the resulting colder winters and hotter summers would make the world a much more hostile place for most of us to live in?

Trevor:   They would indeed!

Editor:   Because the heat exchange process is so important, let us explore it a little further. One implication of what you have said is that heat can flow across the air/sea interface in either of two directions: whilst heat sometimes flows from the ocean to the atmosphere, at other times it flows from the atmosphere to the ocean?

Trevor: That is correct. The physical principle is that heat always flows from the hotter object to the cooler one.

Editor: So the *direction* of heat transfer may vary with time, and with the local surface and air conditions.... I suppose, therefore, that the *rates* of heat transfer vary too?

Trevor: Yes, they vary widely. And over oceans they are influenced not only by thermal gradients, but also by how rough the surface waters are.

Editor: You mean to say that the rates of exchange are more rapid if the sea is rough?

Trevor: Yes, they are. Waves can be thought of as very local roughenings of the sea surface. We find that these are centres of relatively rapid vertical heat transfer.... and, incidentally, moisture transfer too.

Editor: One result must be that the rough seas around our coasts in winter must warm the air more than calm seas would do, and prompt slightly warmer weather than we would have otherwise! Not being a very good sailor, I am relieved to think that waves may actually have some *benefits* for us. There is nothing I like less than a rough sea when I am on a ship!

Trevor: And I have been just as delighted myself to discover that rough times in our *personal* lives can bring benefits, too!

Editor: Now you have me really puzzled - but intrigued! Please explain.

Trevor: Well, I can remember a time when I was under a great deal of stress in my job. Things deteriorated whilst I spent six weeks at sea on a research vessel on the North Sea. Life at sea is quite unlike the routine at home, and, on that occasion, it got quite depressing! Then, when I got back to shore my job description changed somewhat, pressuring me with new and additional responsibilities. To make matters worse, at about the same time injuries and illness in my family occurred, and further added to the stress. I guess many people have found such changes, or combinations of circumstances, to be very destabilising. They can so easily threaten personal relationships with one's colleagues at work.... with one's wife and family.... even with God! I began to be conscious of effects like this in my own life.

Editor:  You speak of a *"personal relationship with God."* Many people do not have a personal relationship with God at all. Is your personal relationship with Him strong?

Trevor:  Yes, it is, and usually I feel *close* to Him! Ever since my teens, I've enjoyed knowing Him, as it were, as a loving heavenly Father. I've long been conscious that He cares for me, and has been guiding my life.... much as any loving, caring father would try to guide the lives of his children.

Editor:  But you seem to be suggesting that the stresses of life can sometimes disturb that kind of relationship?

Trevor:  Absolutely - especially when we're affected by several different types of stress at once! But it is great to realise that the Christian's personal reliance on God can actually be *enhanced* through such periods of stress. Certainly, the greater the pressure from outside, the more obvious it is that we need God's help if we are to withstand, and even overcome that strain. Just as children need the help of their parents most when danger threatens, so in times of difficulty, when we find ourselves under increased pressure, we Christians have to rely on God even more than usual. And at such times it is really encouraging to realise that God has brought many people through much rougher times than we often experience ourselves.

There is also another point related to this discussion which occurs to me from my air/sea interaction work. The worst seas for sailing are those affected simultaneously by both *waves* - which are the result of local wind stress on the sea surface, and *swell* - the result of wind stress on the surface somewhere else! This is because patterns of waves and swell often cut across each other. Then the sea surface can be both rough, and very confused. As an oceanographer, though, I know that it is precisely in such sea conditions that heat exchange - which we talked about earlier - can be most rapid. It is in these areas that the air above the sea can benefit most, by being warmed even more than usual.

I would suggest that it is like this in life, too. It is when personal stress levels are highest, when life seems roughest and most confused, that God can most effectively warm us with His love - and, as it were, transfer to us even more of His care and concern than when life is relatively tranquil.

Editor: And once calm has been restored, we have *benefited from the storms* - rather like air which has gained extra energy from a previous period of rough weather?

Trevor: That's right! That's just how it can be.

Editor: I have one last question. You are a physical scientist, with a high and well-deserved international reputation; and a most responsible leadership role, yet you also clearly have a strong personal faith in God. Is it not *difficult* for someone in your position to believe in Him?

Trevor: Certainly not! Indeed, I reckon that the more knowledge we have of the Universe, the *easier* it should be to believe in God! Let me explain how this is the case for me. In the last few minutes I've spoken mostly about stress features - essentially *irregular* disturbances of the sea surface, like waves and swell. But we could equally well have used this time to talk about more *regular* cycles of sea surface change - the tides. Let me simply say that these speak to me of a beautiful - and beneficial - basic pattern in the behaviour of the oceans of the world. This regularity, and many others at different scales throughout the Universe, speak to me of design, and therefore of a great Designer, namely God.

Many features of God's creation can speak to us of God Himself. Let's mention a few more. I have to confess that there are some things we understand relatively poorly in oceanography - for example the currents which lie well below the surface. These are often quite slow and appear inconsequential. However, as I mentioned earlier, we increasingly believe that the deep ocean has very important influences on our environment as a whole. Indeed its influences are probably much larger-scale and longer-term than those of waves, or swell, or tides. These deep oceanic currents speak to me of *God's underlying influence on the whole of human history*! This influence may not always be very obvious - but it is there, nonetheless, underpinning everything else.

So, the more I see and understand of the air and oceans, the
more I am convinced of, and marvel at, the great intelligence
that brought them into being.   That intelligence can only
belong to God.   And if He can organise things as great and
powerful as the atmosphere and the oceans, I for one am more
than happy to let Him direct and control something as tiny as
my own life!

# 17.

# THE 'JESUS NUT'

**Phillip Fougere**
(*Regional Technical Manager, Helicopter Manufacturer, Singapore*)

*Singapore is a dynamic, cosmopolitan city at a major crossroads of south-eastern Asia. A premier trading centre, it is also a hub for many international companies and therefore a temporary home for many foreign national experts.*

**Phillip Fougere** *is one of these. Born in Canada, Phillip moved to England when only two years old. On leaving school, he trained as an avionics engineer in the British Army Air Corps, graduating top of his class at the Army School of Electronic Engineering. After Army service in Malaysia, Singapore, Nepal and the UK, Phillip began work with a leading US helicopter manufacturer. For several years past he has been based in Singapore, and is responsible for helicopter supply, service and support operations across a wide region of southern and south-eastern Asia, Australasia and the western Pacific.*

*During a stopover en route from a scientific assignment in Australia, the Editor was able to visit Phillip and his family in Singapore, and learn something not only about helicopters, but also about Phillip's own life too. It was in the course of a conversation recorded for use in the Slavic Gospel Association's "Radio Academy of Science" programme that Phillip first referred to the 'Jesus Nut': not, in this case, someone crazy about Jesus Christ, as the English pun suggests.... for this is also the colloquial name sometimes given to a*

*vital part of a helicopter! Read on, and you will see why this part is*
*so named - and why Phillip argues that trusting and following Jesus*
*Christ is much more sensible than ignoring Him.*

———————————

Editor:   Phillip, welcome!  In the 14 years of transmission of the
            RADAS programme - perhaps reflecting my own enthusiasm
            for air travel - we have met with fixed-wing aircraft
            engineers, and aero-engine designers, but you are the first
            *helicopter* expert we have interviewed.  So I, for one, shall be
            specially interested in what you have to say.  You have
            worked with helicopters for many years now, I believe?

Phillip:  Yes, I guess, about 30 years in all.  I first became interested
            in them when I was serving in the British Army.  This has a
            large number of helicopters, mainly for airborne observations,
            communications and transport.  Then I took a job at what is
            called the 'Aeroplane and Armament Experimental
            Establishment'.  This is located at an airfield which became
            famous as a 'Battle of Britain' base in World War II,
            Boscombe Down in southern England.  My next employment
            was in civil aviation with a charter and air-taxi company.  I
            then joined Bristow Helicopters, one of the largest helicopter
            operators in the world.

Editor:   Your job with them, if I remember correctly, was mainly in
            support of the oil industry in the North Sea?

Phillip:  Yes, and I spent a lot of time on the off-shore oil production
            platforms, helping to ensure that the oil company helicopters
            - which are vital links between the rigs and the mainland -
            were fully serviceable.

Editor:   And now for several years you have served as a technical
            expert in avionics for one of the world's largest helicopter
            manufacturers, based here in Singapore.  Do you travel much
            in the course of this work?

Phillip:  Sometimes, yes.  This last year, for example, I've flown with
            one of our new helicopter models across most of south-
            eastern Asia, from the The Philippines to India.  That trip had
            some exciting moments!  We looked down into the new crater

of the volcano Mt. Pinatubo in The Philippines.... were grounded by bad weather on a hilltop in southern India.... and had some fascinating moments dodging condors, birds with three-metre wing-spans!

Editor: Never a dull moment, for sure! But tell us in layman's language, what does 'avionics' involve?

Phillip: Avionics is concerned with aircraft instrumentation, communication, navigation, and control.

Editor: I am sure that it is a fascinating subject in its own right. But, to the layman - and in this context I am well qualified to speak as one myself! - the greatest source of fascination with helicopters is not how they are controlled, but how they fly. Rather like the bumble bee, which seems far from aerodynamic, helicopters do not look the right shape to stay in the air. Can you tell us, in a nutshell, how and why helicopters fly differently from fixed-wing aircraft?

Phillip: Well, I'll try!
For any aircraft to fly, it must have some means of 'lift'. One way this can be achieved is by inducing movement of air across a specially-engineered wing - technically known as an 'aerofoil'. In the case of a fixed-wing aircraft this flow of air is achieved by propelling the whole aeroplane forwards. In the case of a helicopter, though, the flow of air is achieved by rotating aerofoil blades - the main helicopter rotor. This arrangement gives the helicopter its chief advantages over almost all fixed-wing aircraft: its abilities to fly vertically, and to hover.

Editor: If I understand you correctly, you are saying that the rotor is not only the helicopter's main propeller, but also its wings?

Phillip: That is right! And as such the whole engine, engine shaft, and rotor assembly has to be a complex, closely integrated, and extremely sophisticated, piece of engineering. The *downside* of this type of structure is that flying a helicopter is a much more difficult skill than flying a fixed-wing aircraft.

Editor: And just sometimes, as with fixed-wing aircraft, the skill of the helicopter pilot is not high enough to prevent an accident! The *"Flight International"* magazine I subscribe to suggests that some recent helicopter accidents have been caused by the failure of some single system or component - and that the chance of this happening is higher, and the likely result more often catastrophic, in the case of a helicopter than a fixed-wing aircraft. Could you comment on this, please?

Phillip:   Yes, and I must agree with you. The reason is because, in helicopters, things we call 'non-redundant' features are much more complex than in fixed-wing aircraft.

Editor:    I am interested in your use of the term 'non-redundant'. Are you suggesting that some components in aircraft have no 'back-ups' - that is to say, there is nothing else to do their job if they fail?

Phillip:   Yes, I am suggesting that. And there are more of these non-redundant features in helicopters than in normal aircraft. To make matters even worse, helicopter components are also much more susceptible to catastrophic failure if they become damaged. For example, a fixed-wing aircraft may continue to fly after substantial damage to a wing. But a helicopter is *most unlikely* to go on flying if there is damage to a rotating wing, that is to say, to a rotor.... or the rotor shaft.... or if there is failure of the 'Jesus Nut'.

Editor:    The *what*? Did you say the 'JESUS NUT'?!

Phillip:   That's right, I did!

Editor:    Whatever is that? And what is its purpose?

Phillip:   It is the main rotor retention nut. It sits on top of the hub into which the rotor blades are installed. And it's a very carefully designed component, made of very specially prepared metal. Its main purpose is to ensure that during flight the rotor blade system remains connected to the rest of the helicopter, through the rotor mast.

Editor:    It is easy to see that this must be an absolutely vital component of a helicopter! But why did you call it the 'Jesus Nut'? Is this its official name?

Phillip:   No, but this is how people in the helicopter business commonly refer to it! You see, it's such a vital part of the helicopter that, if it fails in any way, Jesus Christ is the only One who could save the people in the helicopter....!

Editor:    ....Because the helicopter would then be expected to crash! But you speak of Jesus 'saving people'. You should explain this. The man called Jesus Christ was executed by crucifixion, a long time ago!

Phillip:    Yes, He was, but the Bible tells us that Jesus, being God in
            the body of a man, *rose again from the dead* after His
            crucifixion at Calvary! Even before that, Jesus had confirmed
            His personal uniqueness in many ways. One of these was by
            performing miracles. He also taught us much about the
            whole person and work of God. He stressed the fact that God
            is so concerned for the creatures He made that, as the Bible
            tells us, *not even a sparrow* can fall to the ground without His
            knowledge. And Jesus insisted that human beings, like you
            and I, are worth much more to Him than any sparrow!
            Therefore, He knows when we're in danger.... and He can
            miraculously save people from otherwise certain death, as in
            a bad helicopter crash.... if He chooses to do so.
            But let me say this too. If God can save people when the
            'Jesus Nut' on a helicopter fails, He can surely save people
            from other, less dramatic, but ultimately just as potentially
            fatal, situations, whether they are in helicopters or not.

Editor:     I am sure we have all heard stories of people miraculously
            surviving air crashes! But you are suggesting that God more
            commonly saves people from the consequences of other, less
            exotic, dangers. Please give some examples.

Phillip:    Well, there are many which come to mind. Dangers which
            include widespread social evils such as addiction to drugs or
            alcohol. My own father-in-law was an alcoholic until he
            realised that the power of God which raised Jesus from the
            dead could at least as easily help him overcome such a
            relatively small problem as alcoholism.
            Then there was my own situation: less dramatic and more
            common still, but obviously of great significance to me! I
            wasn't a bad guy. I even attended church, and learnt plenty
            about the personality of God. But I now know that, when I
            was younger, my life was aimless, and heading for spiritual
            disaster. It stayed that way until I realised that I needed to
            know more than just facts about the personality of God: I
            needed to *know the person of God Himself*, and His Son,
            Jesus Christ. In a real sense my life was saved when I
            recognised God had already done much to keep me from the
            worst effects of sin - and would protect me spiritually all the
            time if I really believed in Him, and asked Him for His help

every day.    Now, many years after that life-changing realisation, I'm absolutely sure that, unless we have the 'nut of faith in Jesus Christ' in place in our lives, there's no hope at all that we will succeed in living as God wants us to.

Let me illustrate what I mean from my own case.  I used to believe, mistakenly, that I was spiritually safe because I often practised religious ritual.    But mere ritual alone is meaningless!  I'm glad I came to realise there was no way I could please God just because of who I was, or what I did.  It was then that I first sought His help.  You see, it is who GOD is, and what HE can do for *us*, which really matters!  I've been conscious that God has given me His help ever since that time.  I know I'm always safe in His care.

Editor:    Phillip, thank you for these personal and practical thoughts. We would do well to remember them next time we see a helicopter aloft - or maybe even ride in one!  I shall certainly think more about the 'Jesus Nut'.... and thank God that my life like yours, is safe because I am trusting Him to hold my life together.    But allow me one last quick question.    The principles of helicopter flight and engineering seem very technical and complicated: how about the principles of faith in Jesus Christ?

Phillip:    At some levels both these sets of principles are very complicated and difficult to understand.  But the *results* of both can be enjoyed by people who *scarcely understand the principles at all*!

I am sure that few helicopter passengers understand the principles of flight, or helicopter construction: but all these people believe that, if the manufacturer's instructions are faithfully carried out, the helicopters won't let them down.

Meanwhile, not even the most talented, or knowledgeable, expert in Theology fully understands God, or exactly how and why faith in Him is possible.  But, in its essentials, faith in God is so simple that even children and completely uneducated people can understand it, and act upon it.  And the final bonus is this: faith in God is so well-founded that if we trust Him, and obey Him completely, He will NEVER fail us, in any way at all!

# 18.

## THE BEST HELP FOR AIDS PATIENTS

**Dr. Eugen Koh**
(*Houseman, Monash Medical Centre, Melbourne, Australia*)

*One of the greatest tragedies of the Twentieth-Century world has been the appearance and spread like wild-fire of the disease called 'AIDS' - the Acquired Immune Deficiency Syndrome. This scourge, initially and still predominantly of homosexual communities, has shown that it can affect heterosexuals too, and from its first recognition in the 1970s, has multiplied so fast that today it is estimated that over four and a half million people around the world now suffer from it. The effects of AIDS, both on its victims, and their families and friends, are almost always highly traumatic. They usually involve some selection from, or mixture of, guilt, blame, reproof and depression.... in addition to the more direct physical results of this disease including increasing susceptibility to illness, intensifying pain and weakness as it advances, and finally, the premature death of the victim.*

*In view of the stigma still surrounding AIDS, and the many personal, practical, and psychological problems which hinder its treatment, direct involvement with AIDS patients is still a very special calling. Monash Medical Centre in Melbourne, Australia is one hospital which is trying to improve the care given to these suffering people.* **Dr. Eugen Koh** *has been one of the medical team involved in this important programme. Born into a Chinese family in peninsular Malaysia, Dr. Koh studied in England for his three degrees (in Science, Medicine, and Surgery) before moving to Australia to begin his professional career as a doctor in Melbourne. It was here that Dr. Barrett met and interviewed him.*

*In this Chapter, Dr. Koh explains his special interest in the development of 'palliative care' procedures for AIDS patients and others who are terminally ill.... and why he himself has been keen to give people in these circumstances the best help possible.*

---

Let me tell you about my work in the Monash Medical Centre here in Melbourne, Australia, a city of over three million inhabitants. This is a major city not only by Australian, but also by world standards. My hospital is a major one too, at least on the Australian scale! This hospital has 450 beds, and is Melbourne's main medical teaching complex - where many doctors and surgeons are trained. It is a fine hospital in many ways, with a good staff, and really caring atmosphere.

At present I am working on what we call 'general rotation' - spending time in all the different departments in turn. This is because I am intending to become a General Practitioner, a 'family doctor' as we might say in Australia. For this I need a wide range of experience. However, even family doctors have personal preferences within the work they do, and there is a particular area of medicine which appeals to me more than the remainder of general practice: this is 'palliative care'.

Since this is not one of the best-known areas of modern medicine, I guess some further explanation of it is required. The essence of palliative care lies in general care for the patient whom we do not expect to be able to cure medically or surgically. That is to say, the patient who has a condition beyond our present ability to treat successfully.

Patients with such conditions include some with chronic, though not immediately life-threatening, diseases, but most notably those who are terminally ill. The fastest-growing group of such patients are those with Acquired Immune Deficiency Syndrome, or 'AIDS' as this is commonly known.

At present I am spending a lot of time with AIDS patients. These people are particularly in need of palliative care! One of the greatest recent tragedies in the world as a whole has been the growing epidemic of this viral disease, which fatally damages the immune system of the body, thus lowering resistance to more common illnesses. AIDS is a disease which mostly affects drug addicts, homosexuals and promiscuous heterosexuals. It is easy, therefore, for the community as a whole to adopt a judgemental attitude to AIDS victims, and to think, or even say *"They should have known better: they deserve to suffer"*, and to act accordingly, steering clear of them, not wanting to get involved with them at all. But I am glad to say that here in Melbourne there is a group of Christian doctors and nurses who have organised themselves to give free attention to terminally ill people in their own homes. I am privileged to be able to play some part in this. It is a wonderful ministry, helping to give back to frightened, unhappy people at least some hope, and try to restore some feelings of self-worth. We rarely see any of these folk cured physically. But we have seen miraculous changes in some personally, and even spiritually.

For such a ministry as this, at least two things are necessary: One is a strong belief in the value of each individual, and the other a belief in one's own ability to be able to cope with the despair so often associated with terminal illnesses. Speaking personally, I certainly believe in the potential value of each individual.... but so far as coping with the stresses of this kind of work are concerned, if I have any 'inner strength' for this I cannot claim it is naturally my own. Indeed, I can well remember a time when I could not have faced such situations. Nor, I confess, would I have even *wanted to do so* then!

No, something happened to change me, and my attitudes to others. This was when I became a Christian Believer. Any inner strength I may now have for our palliative ministry to AIDS sufferers is entirely a result of my coming to faith in God.

I must say, too, that since I have become a Christian, I have even felt *obliged* to help folk like the AIDS sufferers, because this question has come to me: *"What would Jesus Christ have done with people like these when He was here on Earth?"* Would He have been judgemental and dismissive of them, as society in general seems to be? I have to answer *"NO!"* When I read the New Testament, and its many accounts of dealings Jesus had with people who had behaved unwisely or irresponsibly, even with people who had ignored God consciously and deliberately and had persistently broken His laws, I find that Jesus always had compassion on them.... He was always ready to forgive them.... and He would then help them practically, if they asked Him to do so.

I have to admit that there are many times when trying to show the love of Christ to basically hopeless people is really tough. But for me the heart of the Christian faith is that because the same Jesus Christ who so remarkably helped people in New Testament times is alive today, He can - and wants to - work in and through those who believe in Him. So I am assured that, if I have any inner strength at all to help me in such difficult circumstances, this is one of God's gifts to me, something I have only had since I myself became a Christian. That is why I have to say that becoming a Christian has had such a big influence on me, and the work I seek to do.

But, you may wonder, how did all this happen?

I was born of ethnic Chinese parents in a small town in the Republic of Malaysia, in south-east Asia. My parents paid lip-service to one of the indigenous religions of that part of the world, saying they believed its tenets - but not living as if they did. In that religion there is a clearly identified prophet, but its god is conceptualised only as some rather obscure 'greater goodness'. Indeed, this entire religion is not so much a way of life as a way of *thinking*.... being not so much practical, as *philosophical*. I read a great deal about it as I progressed through school. In many ways it seemed comforting, because it contains few rules and regulations. But for the same reasons it is not very challenging either, because it leaves individuals to determine their actions and reactions for themselves!

Then the time came when I was sent to England to continue my education. I spent five years at a boarding school in the west of England, then five years at King's College, part of the University of London. It was there that I won my degrees in Natural Science, Medicine and Surgery. And it was during that whole time in England that I first came into contact with Christians, whose lives I found very challenging. All this culminated whilst I was working as a research assistant in Cellular Physiology in a large English hospital. The project focussed on how the cells in the body communicate with one another. Through that research I became really impressed with both the complexity of life - and the inadequacy of Science to fully comprehend it.   I cannot go into the details here: they are very technical!  Suffice it to say, I became increasingly convinced that there must be aspects of the problem no-one had yet begun to explore.... there must be facts and explanations totally outside the body of existing theory.... and so I began to wonder: *"Were we approaching the unanswered questions in the right way?"*

In turn, this led me to ask the same question in respect to my own approach to religious and spiritual problems too.

To clarify the issues I began to explore faiths other than the unsatisfying one with which I had grown up: alternative ways of rationalising how the whole complex Universe had come into being.... who we are.... and why we are here.   After much searching, I concluded that the *only convincing explanations* were in the Christian Bible!

From the Bible I learnt that God created everything, for His own pleasure.  But I discovered too, how men and women - God's most intelligent creations - soon came to think of themselves as superior to God Himself.  It became clear to me that some of the results of this incredibly mistaken thinking were to be found in hospitals all over the world!  And it was with great amazement, as I read on in the Bible, that I found that God remains loving and compassionate despite all our insulting behaviour.  He cares greatly for people who have rejected Him.  Most amazing of all, I learnt that we arrogant, misguided people can get to know this all-powerful yet caring God ourselves.  Indeed, He is a God who really wants us to know Him personally, not least so that He can help us, and cure us of our spiritual ills - though not always of our physical ills.

I was very conscious that there are many people today who say *"All this is fine in theory, but the REALITY is different!"*  So I began to search out evidence one way or the other.  And as I did so it became more and more clear to me from the lives of many of my friends and colleagues in England that the Biblical account was not mere philosophy, like the faith of my family.  Instead, the Bible message was practical, powerful, and effective, actually making big differences to people when they acted on it!  These differences were not only *external*, evident through the things they did, but also *internal*, radically affecting the ways they thought about God, about others, and about themselves.   In the face of such overwhelming evidence, I became increasingly convinced that Christianity is a faith that truly works.

Soon I came to the point where I had to try it myself. To be honest, the early changes I felt within myself were not so much dramatic as slow and progressive. But after I first asked God to forgive my neglect of Him, to help me live my life more as He wanted, and to lead me deeper into spiritual truth, I knew that all these requests were being answered.

But there must have been related changes in my own personality too, and in the ways I reacted to different situations. For, on my next visit home, my family quickly realised something had happened to me. They were shocked when I told them that I had turned away from their traditional faith to one they did not understand. But perhaps the most unexpected response was that of one of my aunts who burst out *"But how COULD you become a Christian - you're a SCIENTIST!"* You see, I had never thought this might be thought to be a problem! Indeed, as I have explained, I had searched systematically for a faith that was intellectually as well as spiritually satisfying, and it was through this process that I had found Christianity to be the only religion which provided logical answers to the most basic questions, including those about the Universe, and all life in it. These answers are contradicted neither by the scientific method, nor by any existing scientific knowledge.

So, there is my personal story, much condensed! Maybe, though, there is one last question I should try to address: one which brings together my personal knowledge of God, and the work I am now trying to do amongst people who have lost hope in life. The question is this: *"What is the best help people with terminal illnesses, carrying strong social stigmas - like AIDS - can be given?"*

Undoubtedly it is important to help such folk recover senses of self-worth and self-esteem. In these respects everyone is potentially recoverable, the down-and-outs and drug addicts as well as the terminally ill, because spiritual health can be achieved irrespective of the state of the human body. Indeed, some of the spiritually most beautiful or powerful people in history have been some of the poorest, weakest, and illest of society. Everyone is valuable, equally valuable, in the sight of God! God himself says in the Bible, in Paul's Second Letter to the Corinthians Chapter 12 and Verse 9: *"My power is made perfect in (your) weakness"*. The key to personal change is the recognition that God sent Jesus Christ into the world to pay the penalty for the sins of us all. He loves us all, and wants us all to get to know Him for ourselves. If we do this, we can enjoy His company, and make our lives a success, even when measured by His stringent standards.

So, in conclusion, I want to say that it is only when broken people realise they are valuable in God's eyes that they can begin to rebuild their self-esteem. There have been times in my hospital work when I have really despaired for some individuals, only to see them become dramatically changed - their confidence and poise improving out of all recognition - once they have come to know God through faith in Jesus Christ. Meanwhile, others we have worked with have remained tragic cases, because they have not taken that step of faith in God. But we still have to go on loving even these, and caring for them, unconditionally, not least because this is precisely what God does for each of us - until we respond to Him positively, or tragically, lose for ever the opportunity to change our relationship with Him.

# 19.

## THE BIG MATCH: GOOD VS. EVIL!

**Rodney Neal**

(*Senior Civil Engineer, Australian Government, Sydney, Australia*)

*It is not often the Editor makes new friends at breakfast.... indeed, now his children are adults, he rarely sees anyone other than his wife at that meal! However, overseas travel opens up a wide range of unusual opportunities to socialise. One such opportunity presented itself during Dr. Barrett's last scientific visit to Australia. In many of the main Australian cities* "Business Men's Breakfasts" *are held regularly for professional people who have found faith in God, or who are interested in trying to find such a faith for themselves. It was at one such Breakfast in Sydney over fruit juice, bacon and eggs, and toast (all things he would not normally have for breakfast at home!), that Dr. Barrett met* **Rodney Neal**, *and Rodney promised to mail him the story of how he had come to find God for himself for use in the RADAS programme.*

*At last, with an apology for the delay, the script arrived. This Chapter is a very modestly edited version of it.*

*Rodney Neal is a Senior Civil Engineer with an Australian Government organization based in Sydney. This provides a range of advisory and practical support services to major national and international civil engineering projects, including port and airport planning and construction, design and implementation of defence bases, major road developments, and many more.*

*But even such down-to-earth people as Civil Engineers ask themselves questions about the most important goals in life. In this brief, but succinct, autobiography Rodney explains how he identified goals for himself, then set out to achieve them. However, as he sought for them he became acutely conscious, too, of the great battle raging all round us in the world: the* battle between good and evil....

---

A few years ago I knew that I had achieved all the goals I had previously set for myself in life. I had a wonderful wife, two daughters and a son, a large new family home, a new car and a good job. I was not a millionaire, but I certainly was not short of money.

Maybe it was because I had achieved so much of what I had always hoped for that I suddenly began asking myself if there could be other goals for which I should aim too. But I could see none that had any real worth or meaning, apart from maintaining those I had already strived successfully to achieve.

So, I asked myself, what was there to worry about? I had life insurance, home insurance, car insurance, health insurance, and superannuation. It occurred to me that if we put such high values upon life, this must be *precious*. But this did not square with my long-held belief that there was no real or lasting purpose for life. It was at this point that I began to sense there was something missing, both from my understanding of what life is about, and from my own life itself. If this were so, then I had to do something about it quickly, for life is obviously easy to lose, whether by accident, sickness, act of crime, violence or even war. Several incidents sprang to mind where I myself had already come close to death.

Twice I had been involved in near head-on collisions on country roads.

Once a petrol bowser had blown up just a few metres away from me.

Once I nearly electrocuted myself trying to fix a TV set.

On another occasion three men, though unprovoked, had attacked me, punching me and throwing me to the ground.

Recollecting this last event in particular triggered other questions in my mind. Why should some people seem to want to hurt, or even end the lives, of others? Are men and women merely animals? Can we truly distinguish good from evil? Supposing we do know the difference, why is it that some people are criminals, choosing to harm others, rather than helping them? Indeed, broadening the argument to include all obvious forms of wrong against fellow human beings, why is it that many people seem to deliberately choose evil instead of good?

I recalled from my childhood and teenage years that the churches I had been sent to by my parents had taught the existence of 'Satan', a great, personal, evil being in the world. It now seemed to me that mankind alone, imperfect though we surely are, could not possibly be responsible alone for the many atrocities of history: for racial exploitation and even genocide.... for the extermination during World War II of millions of Jews.... for Pol Pot's 'killing fields' in Kampuchea.... for all the destruction, and deep national and personal tragedies, of war. I became sure that there must be a spirit of evil active in the world which urges men and women, and even many young people, boys and girls to do wrong.

As I pondered these things, my train of thought developed further. By himself, unchallenged or unopposed, one supernatural being who was evil would totally dominate merely mortal men and women. However, we also see much *good* in many people. Therefore, just as evil, and its author Satan, are real, circumstances insisted to me that a supernatural being who is good must be real, too! I recalled from my church attendance earlier that Christians call such a being 'God'.

It was at this point that I came suddenly and unexpectedly to the recognition of a new goal, a new ambition, for my life: I wanted to achieve something that would be truly praiseworthy, having a lasting beneficial effect on the world. But how could I do this? I was sure I could not become a great explorer, politician, or philanthropist. If I bequeathed money from my will for some kind of prize, the capital would soon become exhausted, and the good it could do would evaporate. One thing I must emphasize: at *that* stage I did not want God to feature in my plans. Indeed, my recent conclusion that He - as the source of all that was truly good - must be real had shocked me! I had not wanted to pursue the consequences of that conclusion any further.

Now the Bible pictures God as being made up of three persons, each with a distinctive area and type of activity. *First*, God the Father. *Second*, God in human form - the Lord Jesus Christ, the One Who lived on Earth to become the Saviour and Redeemer of mankind. And *third*, the Holy Spirit, the active presence of God moving amongst the people of the world today.

There is a famous Christian poem by Francis Thompson called *"The Hound of Heaven"*. This takes its inspiration from Bible verses which speak of the Holy Spirit actively following and seeking out people to bring them back to Himself. Looking back, it is as if God knew I was afraid to search for Him. Instead, His Spirit, like the bloodhound trained to search out a lost person, or escaped criminal, pursued and tracked me down, until I could escape no longer, either from God Himself, or from His claims on my life. One evening in 1985 our home was visited by two young guys from a local church. They enquired if I would be interested in coming to attend their church services. Slightly embarrassed, I replied obliquely that I had been thinking of sending my eldest daughter to Sunday School - just as I myself had been sent when I was young!

To my surprise the pastor of the church then began to visit us. So my inner debate resumed, aided by the pastor's good knowledge of the Bible. I was interested to hear that Satan himself knows that God is real, and that, as the Letter of James Chapter 2, Verse 19 says, this knowledge *makes Satan's demons fear and tremble!* It was even more thought-provoking to realise that Satan also knows that Jesus Christ is the Son of God who came to Earth to pay, through His death at Calvary 2000 years ago, the rightful penalty for every wrongful deed of the whole human race, past, present and future. This was something most men and women clearly have not recognised. It was something I myself had not understood before. The pastor explained that, acting on the knowledge of who Jesus is, and accepting what He did for us, frees any of us from our evil past. It also makes it possible for us to serve God and so do good, rather than continuing, even if unconsciously, to reject Christ and serve Satan, which is to continue to do evil in the sight of God.

As a Civil Engineer I am used to acting as far as possible within the realms of what we see, know, understand, and can put practically to the test. Thinking I was moving out of my depth in our discussions with the pastor, I asked him how I could be really sure that Jesus is the Son of God and rose from the dead as the Bible asserts. His answer was simple, based on the theme of Psalm 34 which is: *"Test Him and see!"* This appealed to my practical nature: if Jesus really is the Son of God, then as we pray to God in the Name of Jesus, God will answer! I knew

I must pray to God and claim forgiveness through His death on Calvary's cross for all I had done wrong.

Doing this was to be the turning point of my life - and my wife's life too, for she prayed in the same way. Since that time many things have made much more sense than they had ever done before.

One of these is the physical Universe. Many scientists puzzle and argue over the origin of the Universe, the origin of life on Earth, and the origin of the human race. But the Christian knows that nothing could have existed if God had not created it, that is to say, if He had not brought it into being literally *out of nothing*! For this is the meaning of the Ancient Hebrew in which the Biblical book of Genesis was first written. So the Christian appreciates that it was God Who created all life on planet Earth, along with its marvellous diversity of creatures, and the complexity of the ecosystems into which they fit. I now marvel at the truth that, just as God has made every atom and every star, He makes each person individually. Comparing my work - designing roads, drains and airfields, all things that are comparatively small and temporary - with His work as the designer and builder of the physical Universe, makes me personally all the more appreciative of His *astounding* might, wisdom and power.

But since I found God for myself, through my first simple, yet sincere, prayer to Him, the spiritual Universe has made much more sense too. A key player in it is Satan. Satan too, is very real, and tries to divert our attention away from God. But when I found God I became sure that here was the One Who alone could enable me to fulfil my new ambition: the ambition to achieve something that would have a good and lasting effect for eternity. You see, I have come to realise that the highest calling in life, as the great Christian pioneer Paul once put it in his Letter to the church of the Colossians, Chapter 1, Verse 10, is to *"Live a life worthy of the Lord,"* and which will *"please Him in every way."*

In the plan and providence of God living such a life may involve great acts of goodness which will be widely recognized as benefiting maybe even much of the human race. More likely, though, it will involve relatively local, even individually-orientated, deeds of kindness and value. Since God is the One who opens all such doors of opportunity, and gives the strength to do what is right, we cannot complain, whether our personal calling attracts widespread human acclaim - or, conversely, escapes public recognition! God requires only that we serve Him as faithfully as we can - and it is through doing this that we will achieve what is good and lasting in His sight. Of this I am now fully certain.

I hope you too, will put this to the test, shunning Satan, renouncing all your sins. If you seek God, His free forgiveness, and His plans for your own life as I have done, I am certain you will not be disappointed, but will find that deep sense of personal fulfilment which I now enjoy. It is to that end that I have been glad to set down my own experiences, telling the story of Christ, in Whom *"We have redemption through His blood, the forgiveness of sins."* (Paul's Letter to the Ephesians, Chapter 1, Verse 4).

# 20.

# DENYING THE 'GREAT REAPER IN THE SKY'

**David Jordan**
(*Senior Equipment Engineer, Toulouse, France*)

*The title of a recent British television series was* "Your Life in Their Hands". *It featured the efforts of surgeons to correct a wide range of physical defects, or a multiplicity of diseases, in their patients. Perhaps such a series should acknowledge also the work of the operating theatre support teams who prepare each patient for surgery, or perform vital tasks during an operation.*

*This chapter features* **David Jordan,** *an electronics expert now working for Motorola, an international applied science company in Toulouse, France, where he is supervising the installation of equipment to prepare silicon chips for use in a new range of computers. However, David's most advanced training, in the University of Wales, was in Applied Biology, and focused on electronic involvements in human surgery. Putting this training to practical use, David worked until recently as an important member of a hospital operating theatre team in Bristol Royal Infirmary - the largest state-run hospital in south-west England. As part of a team specialising in open heart operations, he was often in a position to say to his patients* "Your heart will be in the surgeon's hands - but your LIFE will be in mine!!"

*David and his wife Lydia still own a house close to the Barretts, and return home from time to time to see their children and friends. On one such visit the Editor was able to meet with David again, and update this conversational script, first used in RADAS broadcasts in the late 1980s.*

*So, let us meet David Jordan to learn of the work he did in Bristol as a 'clinical perfusionist'.... and to discover how David coped when, very recently, he found himself on the way to the operating theatre, not as a member of the medical team, but as a* patient!

---

Editor:   David, I am sure others will want to know exactly what 'clinical perfusion' involves.   I guess this is not a term in everyday use outside the hospital environment!

David:   'Clinical perfusion' is the science of keeping a human being, or a human organ - some vital part of the human body like the heart, lungs, liver or a kidney - alive during surgery, and until surgery can be completed.   Or after an accident or other trauma, until repairs have been effected, or the system has been stabilised again.  So, put as simply as possible, the aim of the clinical perfusionist is to *maintain life through some life-endangering episode.*

Editor:   We know you have worked in the Cardiac Unit of a major hospital.   In what way were you yourself responsible for maintaining the life of a patient during something as serious as heart surgery?

David:   I was responsible for the running of a 'heart-lung machine'. This is a very complex apparatus.   Its main purpose is to take over the function of the heart and lungs while surgical procedures are being carried out on the heart.   But also, to do these things, many aspects of the state and condition of the body have to be continuously monitored, and I was responsible for this too.

Editor:   Tell us some of the parameters the clinical perfusionist has to monitor during heart surgery.

David:   He - or she - has to monitor *blood pressure*, both the 'arterial' blood pressure - which has to be measured in three ways -

and the 'venous' blood pressure. He has to check regularly the *temperature* of the body, and of the brain and, of course, of the myocardium - the outer layer of heart muscle. He has to watch the *rates of supply* of vital body fluids, and the body fluids lost by suction as the operation proceeds. The clinical perfusionist is also responsible for an *electrocardiogram*, which logs the rate of the heart-beat, or 'pulse' as we often call it, and the wave form of each and every individual heart-beat.

Editor:  It is easy to see how you can claim that the patient's life is in the hands of the clinical perfusionist! But what kinds of patients have you helped? Tell us some of the categories of people you have helped keep alive when you worked at Bristol Royal Infirmary.

David:  I have had many different kinds of patients! They have included day-old babies, found with serious defects at birth. And somewhat older patients, for example those with 'holes in the heart'. Also we often treated patients from early middle age who had developed circulatory faults, such as damaged heart valves, the results of rheumatic fever. Then, especially amongst the older age groups, we conducted many coronary by-pass operations, replacing hardened arteries with veins grafted from the legs.

Editor:  I am intrigued to know what kind of preparation you had for such a highly technical and responsible job. Was it very *specific* training?

David:  Not in the academic sense, no. You see, such a job is *very specialised*, both technically and medically. There's no course of study anywhere in the United Kingdom which offers all the training needed for it. So, there is only one place where you can really learn to cope with a job like this - in the operating theatre itself!

Editor:  Did you have any other jobs before you became a clinical perfusionist?

David:  Yes, before I began work at the Bristol Royal Infirmary, I worked for Philips.

Editor:  The multinational electrical and electronics company?

David:  Yes, Philips manufactures a long line of products ranging in size and complexity from electric razors, through stereo systems, to baggage-handling X-ray machines at airports.

And it was while I was with that firm that I studied for my degree in electronics at a technical college in South London. Following graduation, I concentrated on servicing video cassette recorders and other types of electronic equipment, before becoming a training instructor to Philips apprentices. At that time I never *dreamt* that I would go on to work in a specialised surgical unit!

But my wife - whom I married in 1970 - is a nurse, and I gradually became more and more interested in medical matters too. Soon I heard of a job vacancy at the Bristol Royal Infirmary - and found myself studying for a further degree, this time in Applied Biology. This helped prepare me for the more purely medical dimensions to my work in the Operating Theatre. But I repeat - most of the skills I have had to use in hospital were acquired 'on the job', as I began to work with the close-knit team in the Operating Theatre itself.

Editor:  I am sure there must be times when all the skill and training in the world cannot save a patient's life. How did your surgical team respond to the death of a patient you tried hard, but unsuccessfully, to help?

David:  Obviously we were all upset at times like that. But we could not let ourselves become *too* upset, or we would not have been able to try again next time we were in theatre. So we had to train ourselves not to become too involved emotionally with the patients, or indeed with the job itself.

Instead, we had to encourage each other, by remembering that we always expected to *win* more battles than we lost.

However, I was always interested in the responses of my colleagues when one of our patients died. Although most of the people I worked with were atheists or agnostics, almost inevitably someone would say then: *"That's another one for the Great Reaper in the Sky!"*

I remember one particularly bad week we had in theatre. One day someone announced the score: *"Surgeons 1, Great Reaper 3!"* Although that someone was not a Christian, he spoke the truth, for whereas in one sense the patients were in *our* care, it is even more true to say that they were *in the hands of God*, and sometimes He would claim more lives than we could restore. For myself, I could accept any outcome relatively easily. After all, every one dies sooner or later: the most that modern medicine or surgery can do is to *prolong* life. Paraphrasing the Bible, *"God gives life"* and, eventually, *"He takes it back again"*!

Editor:     Most of us are relatively happy if we can avoid even *thinking* about dying and death. You must have encountered death much more often than most of us. Did this worry you?

David:      No, it didn't, because I am a Christian Believer. I became one when I was 18 years old. Let me tell you how it happened. Although I had been brought up in a Christian home, by my late teens I had not consciously believed in God for myself. Now 'Communion' services are when Christians particularly remember the death of Jesus Christ, God's Son, on behalf of the whole of sinful mankind. These are specially solemn occasions, for Jesus Himself said that the Communion service *bread* would symbolise His body - which He knew was soon to be broken on a Roman cross. Furthermore, the Communion service *wine* would symbolise His blood - shed, using the imagery of the Jewish prophets of old, to wash away the sins of all who repent of them before God. In Communion services we recognise that, instead of punishing us for our sins, God is ready to accept the death of Jesus as the only penalty which need be paid for them. During one such service I attended, the minister said to the congregation, *"Any of you who know and love the Lord are invited to partake of the Communion bread and wine."*
For the first time in my life, this sudden realisation struck me in a flash: *"I know and love Him - so that means ME!"* Although I had reached that point more gradually than many other Christians, I was immediately able to really thank Him for His death at Calvary 2000 years ago, and ask Him not only to cleanse my life from things that displeased Him, but also to help me keep it clean in the years to come.
Today my faith in God is very strong - after all, I have now experienced His companionship and help for many years. And this is why death does not worry me. Indeed, death should hold no fear for any Christian, because the Bible describes death as the Christian's *gateway to eternal life* in God's own home in heaven.

Thus, when a Christian dies on the operating table I am very sorry for the relatives - but very happy for the Christian! For the Bible says that there are ways in which *"As long as we are at home in the body we are away from the Lord."* (Paul's Second Letter to the Corinthians, Chapter 5, Verse 6). No, it was - and is - the *other* patients I am most sorry for: those who die not having made their peace with God. The Bible teaches plainly that, for them, eternity will be never-ending torment. I shudder at the thought!

Editor   I know you recently found *yourself* on the way to the operating table, and that that was a real test of your faith in God. Tell us about it.

David:   About a year ago I developed some symptoms which prompted me to seek advice from our family doctor. After various examinations and tests a malignant tumour was diagnosed. However, the specialist said that the tumour was operable, and that surgery was likely to be successful: after it, the chances of further problems were very small. Of course, the diagnosis had come as a shock, but the fear I began to feel was not a fear of dying. Remember, because of my faith in God I know I will go to be with Him when my body dies. No, my fear was at first a fear of pain, then of being anaesthetised! I was used to working with anaesthetised patients, but I was not used be being a patient myself.

As the time for the operation approached, I was helped by two things. One was a seeming mistake, the other definitely not. The apparent mistake was that I was taken initially to the wrong hospital ward! How was this a blessing? The Ward Sister was a Christian also, and encouraged me with her own faith in God. The other thing which helped me was the knowledge that many Christian friends were praying for me - in England, France, and elsewhere too. I was so glad to be able to entrust myself to the hands of God that, although my 'pre-med' drugs were given to me only five minutes before the anaesthetic was administered - too late for them to be a help - yet I went into the operating theatre totally relaxed, even enjoying the experience of seeing everything from a new perspective. I marvelled at all this. Without my faith in God I simply could not imagine myself coping with such a situation!

And God has been good to me since the operation, too. My post-operative checks have all been clear. The 'Great Reaper' does not wish to harvest me yet.... but when He does, I shall be glad, and ready for His call.

Perhaps, in conclusion I should say this: no surgical procedures can, or ever will, make any difference to the health of the *soul*. Only God can heal this. Our atheistic and agnostic friends in the medical profession often cover their disappointment when they lose a patient by speaking of the 'Great Reaper in the Sky', but the Bible never speaks of God in this way! Rather, His Son, Jesus Christ is sometimes called the 'GREAT PHYSICIAN' because He is the One, and the only One, who can heal our souls, and so prepare us to enjoy life with God, not just in this life, but for ever.

# 21.

# LEARNING TO SWIM

**Ashok Jalalabadi**
*(Science Lecturer, Speciss College, Harare, Zimbabwe)*

*This personal story concerns an Indian, **Ashok Jalalabadi**. Ashok grew up in a small village in Bihar State, in India, and through hard work and a series of scholarships, went on to become a Mathematics graduate from the University of Bombay, India. Much of his working life, though, has been spent in Africa, mainly in the southern African republics of Zambia and Zimbabwe. Today he lives with his wife Mary, a horticulturalist, in Harare, the capital of Zimbabwe, where he teaches Physics and Mathematics at Speciss College.*

*It was also in Africa that, through personally observing the lives of Christians, and thinking through all the issues involved, Ashok had what he calls "A life changing experience that I want to share with everyone". This experience has freed him from the greatest fear in his own life, and that of many others: the fear of death. This is how Ashok recounted his personal story recently to Dr. Barrett, who was visiting Zimbabwe under a United Nations Development Programme scheme to train local scientists in the use of satellite data for monitoring the local environment. Intriguingly for a self-professed non-swimmer, Ashok entitles his personal story "Learning to swim".*

Early on the morning of January 8, 1981, I had an experience which was to change my life completely: it was to liberate me from many fears and misconceptions I had had since early childhood.

But first, let me give you some background about myself, and share with you some of the events which led up to that unforgettable event.

I was born into an average Indian family, and brought up in the traditions of one of the local religions. In many ways it seemed an easy going religion - neither too strict nor too extreme. Its 'god' is rather nebulous, having no discernible attributes. Rather, it is an ageless, formless 'universal spirit' which lives far beyond time and space. My childhood religion taught that life on Earth is a testing and preparation ground for eventual one-ness with that universal spirit. Here I had to live my life as best as I could, for, when I died I would be re-born to another life on Earth. This could be either better or worse than the one before it, depending on what I had done in that previous existence. I was taught that the main object of life was increasing improvement through self effort, and devotion to that nebulous divine being, so that my spirit could eventually be set free from that wearisome cycle of life and death.

Unfortunately, the more I thought about this cycle, the more frightened I became! I knew I did not deserve to be reincarnated higher up the scale than I was then. I feared I was not making any progress towards becoming part of the great 'universal spirit'. So I developed an absolute, and very real, terror of death! My religion did not help me in any way to overcome this dread. And I remember lying awake at night thinking how unfair it would be for the rest of the world to carry on after my death as if nothing important had happened - for it would surely do this, because I was not specially significant in any way!

The first inclination I gained that the truth about life and death is very different from this was in 1974. I was teaching Mathematics in Zambia. One of my teaching colleagues there was Richard, an American. Richard had a degree in Industrial Engineering from the prestigious Cornell University in the USA. He was also, I soon discovered, a Christian.

Richard and his wife Kathy began talking to Mary and me about Jesus Christ. They said Jesus had been God in the form of a man, but that He had been crucified for claiming to be God. However, He proved His deity by rising from the dead - a fact observed by many -

and if I trusted Him myself, I would get to know God personally. Best of all, I would then go to live with Him when I died!

I must admit that these ideas did not really appeal to me at first. Christianity required belief in many apparent physical anomalies - like angels.... a virgin giving birth to the Son of God.... and the dead body of Jesus coming to life again in His resurrection. I could not understand how someone like Richard, with a strong technical and scientific background, could believe in things like this! I told him so. We agreed to disagree on the whole subject, and otherwise remained close friends.

Then events led Mary and me on a long round trip: Zambia to England, to India, and back to Zambia over a period of about three years. On our return to Zambia, Richard and Kathy began telling us about Jesus again as if we had never been away! Eventually, towards the end of 1979, Mary announced to me one day that she had become a Christian! This astonished me, because she is British and had been born into a 'Christian' family. I could not understand in what way she had now 'become a Christian' or had been 'born again' as she now claimed: surely she had been a Christian from birth?

What I could understand was that there then followed the worst period in our married life! There was real resentment on my part towards Mary over her increasing involvement in Christian activities, and I am afraid a degree of persecution resulted from me towards Mary. I taunted her about her new faith. I posed questions that she could not answer to my satisfaction, and sometimes even reduced her to tears. However, through it all I could not escape the conclusion that she had become a changed person - and that something had happened to her that gave her real peace and strength, to the point that she neither responded angrily to my taunts, nor retaliated in any way.

I was then offered a teaching post in the neighbouring country of Zimbabwe. Just before leaving Zambia I met the pastor of Mary's church. His name was Joe Simfukwe. Joe was a young Zambian. To my surprise I found I could relate to him easily, as he, too, had a scientific background. Joe had graduated in Biology from the University of Glasgow, Scotland, and had returned to become a Chief Research Officer at the Mount Makulu Agricultural Research Station in Zambia. Once again I could not understand why anyone should act so remarkably: Joe had given up a great scientific career in order to become a full time leader in the Christian Church! I expressed some of my fears to Joe Simfukwe.  He could not answer all my questions to my satisfaction, though he did satisfy many of my doubts about the logic of Christianity.  Then we had one conversation in particular which was to have a lasting impact on me.

Joe knew I was a non-swimmer.  He asked what I would do if I wanted to learn to swim.

*"I would probably get hold of some books on swimming"* I replied.

His next question was whether this alone would enable me to swim.

*"Obviously not!"* I said.

So what would my next step be, he asked.

*"I would probably go and watch people swimming"* was my answer. *"If I thought they were enjoying themselves I would consider the possibility of learning to swim myself.  But I am not sure if I would like it too!"*

Joe observed that this was all ultra cautious: I seemed to want all the answers before I was prepared to get into the water!  Yet, it would be impossible to answer all my questions without getting in.  And, he went on, becoming a Christian can be just the same: we may read books about it, even the Bible itself, and observe others living Christian lives; but a lot of questions about Christianity can only be answered from personal experience.  The only sure way to obtain answers to our questions about the Christian faith is to commit ourselves to God, and to try it out personally.

By the time we left Zambia a few days later, after many more discussions with Joe, I had exhausted all my arguments.  Only a few days after we arrived in Zimbabwe I made my decision to become a Christian.  By accepting Jesus Christ as the only One Who could save me from the consequences of my sins, I had *metaphorically* entered the water and committed myself to a wholly new way of life.  A month later I *physically* entered the water as I was baptised - a symbolic act in obedience to Jesus Christ Who took this ancient rite and said that, for Christians, it would now be one way of showing others that old lives had ended, and new spiritual lives had begun through faith in Him. Wonderfully for me, as I began to learn more about Christianity, the terror I had had of death began to recede.  Life became much fuller and more satisfying as Mary and I learnt together, as it were, the swimming strokes of the Christian life.

Today, I thank God for His perfect timing in allowing my confidence in Him to grow before a traumatic event struck our family and tested our new found faith: our eldest son died after two brain operations for encephalopathy. Stretched out over several months previously were long hours at his bedside. We were afflicted by heartaches and doubts, questions and anger, tears and helplessness, as this little five year old boy of ours fell sick, and suffered much before he died. Yet at the end of it all, after much prayer and fasting, we found we could look back and see that God had been in total control all the time. Though He did not calm the raging storm around us, undeniably He calmed us in the midst of the storm. Through His presence He freely gave us His peace, that peace described in the Bible as *"passing all human understanding"*. Mary and I had come to be sure that God's love extends beyond the death of the body. God's Word, the Bible, assures us that if we all love Him we will be reunited with our loved ones in the life to come. I no longer feared death - I had become sure that for me, as for every Christian, it is the gateway to Heaven!

I have learned also not to mind that life on Earth may carry on after my body dies. Instead, because I know God personally, I look forward to meeting Him face to face in that place where pain, sorrow and tears will be things of the past. I now swim confidently through the waters of life, and enjoy teaching others also how to commit themselves to God through faith in Jesus Christ.

# 22.

# THE IDEAL CITY

Bill McVernon

*(City Works Engineer, Nunawading, Victoria, Australia)*

*Most of the people in the world today are city dwellers - but few of us (or them!) spare much thought for the practical problems of providing and maintaining city environments which are reasonably pleasant for all to live in. It is the responsibility of a few, highly-trained, experts to do their best, often against great odds, to make cities as pleasant and efficient as possible for everyone.*

*Although the popular view of Australia is a country of wide open spaces, the land of the vast and legendary 'Outback', Australia is one of the most highly urbanised countries in the world. So, in order to learn something of what is involved in making and keeping cities convenient for us all, it is not unnatural to turn to an Australian for help.*

*Until his retirement very recently,* **Bill McVernon***, a graduate of the Civil Engineering Department of the University of Victoria, Melbourne, Australia, was Works Engineer for the city of Nunawading, in the State of Victoria. This city is part of the Australian metropolis of Melbourne, which, with its population of over three million and a total area of over 1000 square kilometres, is one of the top ten conurbations of the Southern Hemisphere.*

*The Editor met Bill whilst in Australia to present scientific papers to an International Geographical Union Congress in Sydney, and seminars at the Australian Bureau of Meteorology in downtown Melbourne. One Sunday during his stay in this area, Dr. Barrett and his family helped lead two morning services at a church in Nunawading - and found that they were to be entertained for lunch by the McVernon family. It was after lunch that Bill shared his life-story with the Barretts, in the following way....*

―――――――――――

Let me begin by introducing you to the city of Nunawading. It has a rather strange name, I agree. This is because it is an old name, given to the area by the indigenous Aborigine tribes before white settlement in this part of Australia. Today Nunawading has a population of about 100,000 and an area of some 50 square kilometres. Being only 15 kilometres from downtown Melbourne it is already a fully developed area, being all urban as distinct from rural in character. Most of it is residential, but there are also business districts, some areas of light industry, public institutions such as schools and hospitals, and lots of parkland and playing fields.

Until quite recently my own position in Nunawading was one of considerable responsibility. As Works Engineer I was primarily responsible for a group of over 150 municipal employees - and an annual budget of almost 10 million Australian Dollars, that's to say about $8.5 million US Dollars, or 13 million pounds Sterling!

In these cases all such money comes from taxes, some local, and the rest national. But why so much? Let me outline the things my old Department does.

Its activities are manifold. It constructs and maintains the city roads and sidewalks, sports ovals, car parks and the like. It builds bridges when they are required, tends all the public buildings, and provides much of the so-called 'street furniture'.... road signs, litter bins, bus shelters and so on. To draw an analogy with computing, my Department is concerned with the municipally-provided *hardware* in the city environment, whilst the *software* - mainly flower beds, lawns and trees - is the concern of another group, namely the Parks and Recreation Department! And all of these things - both hardware and software - are planned by the city's Design Department.

Now it is generally agreed that the whole district of Nunawading is really most attractive. I guess I can say that I've personally played an important part in making it a good place to live in, but an even bigger part, I think, in keeping it such a pleasant place: it has been well-managed and maintained for many years. But keeping it pleasant has not been the easiest of jobs! Recent times have seen increasing pressures for change, several of which could be environmentally damaging if allowed to advance unchecked!

For example, our State Government in Victoria has followed a policy of increasing our population. In the case of Nunawading this has only been possible by increasing the population density, placing greater strains upon our roads, schools, hospitals and so on. Some local politicians wanted us to build more factories. But these would have adversely affected services such as water supply and drainage.... and could so easily have made the area less attractive aesthetically. So we resisted them!

Just occasionally I have dreamt of making changes which would create an *ideal* city in Nunawading, indeed turning it into a veritable 'Utopia'. To bring this about, many things would be necessary. Some would be relatively cosmetic, such as improving waste collection and disposal.... improving street lighting.... and upgrading footpaths and keeping them in better repair. But other things would have to be more fundamental, such as providing more recreational facilities.... better shopping facilities.... more centres for the handicapped, old or infirm.... but then the daydreaming has to stop, for the list is endless!

In reality the chances of actually being able to develop our city like this are practically zero! We have neither the space, nor the financial resources, for it. The cost would be astronomical! All politicians are too cautious to promote such improvements.... not least because it is much more common for people in an electorate to re-elect them if they promise not to *increase* taxes, but keep the local taxes *down!*

However, although Nunawading is by no means perfect, I've been glad to continue to live here since my retirement. Our friends are here, the local life-style suits my family, and we are quite close to the church where we've been members for many years. Indeed the church plays an even more important part in our lives now we have retired: we have more time to take part in its different activities.... and have more time to absorb its teaching. And as we get older, we get more and more interested in what the Bible has to say about where we expect to live in the future!

One thing which encourages us enormously is that, whilst I'm sure there is no truly perfect place to live anywhere on Earth, I confidently expect to move to a perfect place, a really Utopian city, after my body dies - the place God has prepared for the souls of folk who have loved and served Him while they have been alive on Earth.

You see, the Bible affirms that God has prepared a *really special* home for them! And by all accounts this is a fantastic place! It is described in the last book in the Bible. This is the book of *"The Revelation"*, a vision of the future given by God 2000 years ago to the Apostle John. The future city in Heaven is described as being really beautiful, with golden streets, and gates studded with precious stones; a city which will be perfectly lit, by the glory of God Himself; and well watered, with a pure crystal stream. But best of all, it is described as a truly happy place, secure from any evil influences; a place where illness, pain, grief and death will all be totally unknown.

Now if this sounds truly 'out of this world', indeed it is. It would be hard to imagine anywhere better! Unfortunately, though, the best things in life always seem to be the most elusive ... and I have to say that entry to God's heavenly city will be *strictly limited*!

Here in Nunawading we do not make any general stipulation on who moves into our city, as long as they can find a home in it. But in Nunadawading, as elsewhere, there is an effective upper limit set upon the population by the size of the city area, and the number and types of dwellings we have in it.

Entry to the heavenly city I've described will be restricted in a very different way. Being God's home, He has not set population quotas, but stringent spiritual standards, for entry into it. So much so that the Bible emphasizes that relatively few people who try to enter will be allowed to do so! This is not because of lack of space, nor because God wants to discriminate in any way against anyone who has ever lived - but because many people, by disobeying and ignoring God, *disqualify themselves* from ever being able to enter it!

What, then, makes me so sure that I myself will be allowed to enter Heaven, whilst most other people will not?

God's book, the Bible, makes me sure! In the Bible, God tells us much about Heaven, and also much about Jesus Christ. The Bible affirms that Jesus was God's own Son, Who, uniquely, lived briefly as a man. This miracle of God entering visibly into our physical world was planned so that other miracles might then be possible. Perhaps the chief of these is that through faith in Jesus Christ, and repentance before God, mere human beings can become God's adopted sons and daughters.... and, therefore, in a legal sense, became brothers and sisters of Jesus Christ Himself. This status secures Christians their future entry to Heaven, for the Bible says that Jesus is the heir to all its wonders and riches, and everyone who has become a brother or sister of Jesus Christ is therefore a joint heir with Him of its many treasures. Because I am a Christian myself, I, therefore, can look forward to the time when my soul will leave this present world: since I am already a joint heir with Jesus Christ myself, a place in the heavenly city is already part of my new inheritance.

Now when we think of all the evil there is in the world, and how all of us as individuals have disobeyed God, it is hard to understand how any of us might be deemed by Him to deserve such preferential treatment! This is why adoption by God is truly a miracle! None of us deserve it, we can't work for it, or even purchase it. We can only receive it as a free gift from God.

But, you may ask, how did I come in to this myself? I had no special advantage or attribute which most people lack. Indeed, when I was younger, I was no different from anybody else: by nature I was nowhere near good enough to deserve entry into Heaven. So, in my own case, gaining God's favour was not something I worked for, and certainly not something I could purchase. But I did reach this most important realisation: that I could never be adopted by God as one of His spiritual children as a result of anything I myself could ever do alone - it was something He offered me, *freely*, if I repented of my sins.

About 35 years ago, when I was a young man of 30, I used to think and question a lot how the world had come about, how it kept going, and what sustained everything. I was professionally interested, of course, in the human environment. I read articles about mankind upsetting its many balances, and the disasters such irresponsible actions often bring about. Like the farmers in parts of America who killed the mountain lions which killed deer. The deer populations then increased. There were then more deer to strip the bark off trees, killing more of them - and causing serious erosion of the soil.

As I thought about these kinds of things I became more and more convinced that there must be a great force, and a super-intelligent brain, behind nature! Everything made too much sense, fitted together far too well, to have come about by chance. I read many different hypotheses of how everything was thought to have evolved, but found none of them convincing. Then I began to read the Biblical explanation. A friend suggested I would find it interesting - and I did! Not only did the Bible insist that the Universe was designed and created by God, whose intelligence is, in the best mathematical sense of the word, *infinite*, but the Bible also made great sense too, when explaining human history.

For example, I had always thought that people, left to themselves, would be, or would ultimately become, really good. I found the Bible argues the reverse! Without God's help, it says, we make an awful mess of everything. There is evidence of this everywhere. So, finally, I came to realise that the Bible account matches perfectly the world I knew and observed all the time.

Then one day I heard a Christian preacher explain a passage in the Biblical Letter to the early Church in Ephesus in Greece. He said that although we have all rebelled against God, any of us can be accepted and approved of by Him! It dawned on me that this passage was telling of the great force who has so remarkably made everything and everybody. But even more amazing for me was the realisation that this great force, this super intelligence, is a PERSON, One who *cares* about us all; One who wants to *help us enjoy* life here; and One Who wants us to *be with Him in Heaven* in the future! It was then that I plead God's forgiveness for all I had previously done wrong, and asked Him to take control of my life. Because He is the great designer, and the source, of life itself, He is obviously much more capable of fashioning our lives than we could ever manage by ourselves! And, remember, the Bible stresses that it is if, and when, we acknowledge His right to control our lives that we become His adopted sons and daughters....

I can say in conclusion that I have never regretted surrendering my life to God's control. Since I did so I have been able to enjoy life much more than I ever did before. And, of course, because God then adopted me as one of His sons, I now have that firm assurance that I will go one day to live in His own home.

Countless millions of others down through the centuries have become joint heirs with Jesus too, and have been similarly assured of a home with Him in Heaven. Life in that perfect city will not cost us anything, for all God's gifts to His children are completely free. He has fully paid for them already. All we have to do is thank Him for them, accept them - then enjoy them to the full! I am in that happy position.

Therefore, although I am now retired, and tangibly growing older every day, I face the future with total confidence, yes, even with eager anticipation.  What I wonder is, can YOU?

# 23.

## SEEING AND BELIEVING

### Dr. Eric Barrett

*(Director, Centre for Remote Sensing, University of Bristol, UK)*


**Dr. Eric Barrett** *is both the editor of this book, and the co-editor (with David Fisher) of its forerunner* "Scientists Who Believe". *A leading international scientist, he holds the very rare distinction of two doctorates. Initially he studied Geography, with Botany and Zoology as subsidiary subjects, for his B.Sc. Honours Degree at the University of Sheffield in northern England, and then researched climatic change for his Master of Science degree at the same institution. In the mid-1960s he became interested in the new field of Satellite Meteorology, and much of his subsequent research has been based on data from Earth-orbiting satellites, including his Doctor of Philosophy thesis entitled* "The Contribution of Meteorological Satellites to Dynamic Climatology." *In 1983 he was awarded his Doctor of Science degree for published work on Environmental Remote Sensing: the citation for this 'higher doctorate' spoke of his* "....sustained and distinguished contribution to geographic science." *In all he has authored or edited some 20 books, plus over 300 scientific papers, articles or reports.*

*Dr. Barrett has held lecturing posts in the English Universities of Sheffield, Leicester and Bristol, plus visiting professorial posts in the Australian Universities of New England and Western Australia. In 1983 he was appointed the first Director of the new Remote Sensing*

*Unit in the University of Bristol. In view of the growing national and international reputation of the Unit, this was upgraded and expanded to a University Research Centre in Remote Sensing in 1995, specialising in Satellite Hydrology and Hydrometeorology, with Dr. Barrett at the helm. He has served on many related committees in the UK and further afield, and as an Expert Consultant to several United Nations agencies, the European Space Agency, the US National Aeronautics and Space Administration, and the US National Oceanic and Atmospheric Administration, as well as several UK and foreign government institutions and commercial companies.*

*Despite all that, Dr. Barrett says that he has always seen scientific work more as a means to an end than an end in itself. Becoming a committed Christian at a young age (as recounted in* "Scientists Who Believe"*), he and his wife Gillian joined the Slavic Gospel Association as Honorary Representatives just before their marriage in 1967. At the request of SGA he designed the new radio programme, RADAS (the* "Radio Academy of Science"*), which began transmissions to the USSR in 1980. Broadcasts of RADAS have continued to the present time, in or to several major countries of the world. Scriptwriting for this programme has brought together his scientific research interests and his missionary concerns. However, Dr. Barrett is firmly convinced that the latter are of much greater importance than the former, for he observes that whilst* "Science is of PASSING significance, because it cannot outlive time, trust in God is of LASTING significance, because it is preparation for eternity.... "*

*In this final chapter Dr. Barrett describes recent health problems he has suffered.... and draws conclusions from them, and the other chapters of this book.*

---

For me, life has been anything but dull since I left school. Studying, then working, in an expanding, interdisciplinary, and international field of science, and simultaneously contributing all I could to the global ministry of a dynamic Christian missionary society, has taken me to over 60 different countries, and to every continent in the world - except Antarctica! It has been my privilege to be in at the birth of many scientific discoveries and technological innovations, and to have worked with almost all the top people in my chosen fields of study. And I like to think that I, too, have been able to make some useful contributions to Climatology, and Environmental Remote Sensing, both fields of growing practical value to mankind as a whole.

During this time there have been many memorable moments. Many things have given me special personal pleasure and enjoyment. As I write, some particularly spring to mind. They include receiving my Bachelor's degree result (with coveted, but rare, First Class Honours).... marrying Gillian (small, dark and attractive but, much more importantly to me, loving, loyal, unselfish and totally supportive).... hearing by telex of the success of my Ph.D. thesis (whilst Gillian and I were aboard the ocean liner *"Canberra"* somewhere on the South Indian Ocean!).... welcoming into our lives our son Andrew (by adoption, at four days notice, when he was one month old).... and greeting our new-born daughter Stella (especially memorable after having been told a few years before that we *"would be unlikely"* to have children of our own!).

I also recall with pleasure many opportunities to work in the 'Third World' for United Nations agencies and national government organisations.... fellowshipping with other Christians everywhere on my travels, but most memorably in places where they were (and in some cases, still are) persecuted dreadfully.... being asked to develop the *"Radio Academy of Science"* (RADAS) programme, at first for broadcasting to the former USSR.... and subsequently interviewing many fellow Christian scientists for it during my travels all around the world.... I have been glad to hear from, or even sometimes meet, folk in far-flung places who said they had been helped by my scientific work, or much better still, who said they had found God themselves through our RADAS programmes, books or audiovisuals.

Trained originally as a Geographer, I have derived particular enjoyment from visiting other countries. I can recall many marvellous and memorable times when travelling, including my first ever trip abroad, as an undergraduate, to beautiful Provence in the south of France.... my first visit to Moscow, including Red Square, and Moscow Baptist Church.... seeing Cape Town's Table Mountain in the early morning, complete with crisp summit cloth of cloud.... being shaken *seven times* in one night by earthquakes in Papua New Guinea.... 'touching base' with the much-fabled and beautiful island of Tahiti in the South Pacific.... passing through the Panama Canal, and helping organise a Christmas Day service two days later on the SS *"Northern Star"*, whilst crossing the Caribbean Sea.... flying the North Polar air route to Alaska, the Arctic ice cap illuminated all the way by the midnight sun.... and exploring Ulan Batar, capital of remote and mysterious Mongolia. I have found myself alone in magnificent places like the deserts of Arabia, and by the Victoria Falls on the border between Zimbabwe and Zambia.... and have explored beautiful islands like the Bahamas and the Canaries with my family. I recall the drama of driving up shapely Mt. Fujiama (*Fujisan*) in Japan; and of breaking through the clouds, aboard a Cathay Pacific Tristar from Tokyo on its final approach to Hong Kong's claustrophobic Kai Tek Airport, and literally gasping with amazement, with other passengers, at the sight of Hong Kong harbour, thick with ships, and fringed by row upon row of spindly sky-scrapers, for all the world like some wierd and wonderful, though foliage-free, forest.

To be truthful, packing all this, and a great deal more, into the last 30 years or so has often left me feeling breathless, even at times quite exhausted! But I have been encouraged by the slow but sure progress with my research projects, and constantly bouyed up by my faith in God. Continuing to see clear evidences of His blessings on us and others, Gillian and I have pressed steadily on.

*              *              *              *

There came a time, though, just when we were optimistic that we might miss many of the worst pitfalls of life's middle years, we began to discover for ourselves that those who love God, and seek to honour Him, are those particularly prone to be targeted by God's great enemy, Satan.

Within a mere couple of years both my parents died: my mother very suddenly and unexpectedly, my father more slowly and agonizingly from cancer. Gillian's mother suffered a series of strokes, none of which were very catastrophic, but all of which were cumulatively disabling. In many ways worse still, our daughter Stella, a very gifted, and until that time, a happy, cheerful and loving person, succumbed to peer and media pressure to develop a lean and hungry 'model' figure - and fell seriously ill with the 'slimmers disease', Anorexia nervosa. This heartbreaking condition, and its common companions, Bulimia and depression, are rightly notorious for the ways they deeply affect not only their immediate victims, but also their families and friends, plus those who try to provide counselling help and support. Imagine our own pain and trauma as loving parents as Stella's illness progressed, with many ups and downs. She spent several periods in hospital, and much of the time we were advised not even to try to give her the love, protection and help any caring parents would have wanted to have done! Those were black days indeed.

Then, in the midst of all these trials, came the day when Gillian and Stella were away attending another sad event for our family: the funeral of the husband of our niece Tania, who had been left a widow at the tender age of 28. At work that day I became aware of some strange visual disturbances in my right eye. I hurried to consult my optician. He did not seem unduly worried, but nevertheless referred me to the Casualty Department at Bristol Eye Hospital, the major specialist centre for eye diseases and defects for the whole south-west of England. To my relief, the Casualty Officer was reassuring: *"You have developed a common problem. You are unfortunate to have developed it so early, but in your case it is benign and does not require any treatment. You will get used to the increased 'floaters' you can see!"*

Unfortunately, the sequence of events which followed did not justify his optimism! Sometimes I have thought that perhaps if I had only delayed my visit to the Hospital by a few more days, many things might have been different. As it was, my eye came to present a changing sequence of visual disturbances. Three months later, whilst at a scientific meeting in the French Pyrenees, I became so concerned about those disturbances that I revisited my optician on returning home. This time he looked grave, and, although it was 5 pm, told me to go back to 'Casualty' immediately. At 8.30 pm my eye was examined by a doctor. That midnight I was admitted to Gloucester Ward (after a quick dash home for pyjamas and washing kit) - and next day I was operated on for attempted repairs to a 'giant tear' in my retina. From my Remote Sensing work (human vision being a natural type of remote sensing!) I knew the retina to be the all-important, image-forming, specialised skin which lines the inside of the eyeball. Apparently the torn retina in my right eye had begun to peel away (or 'detach'), seriously threatening its sight. And, despite the Eye Hospital being a major centre for eye surgery, I was encouraged neither by the news that surgeons there *"Only saw two or three such severe cases every year"*, nor by their advice that *"Giant tears can be very difficult to repair!"*

Over the next three months I was to find how true this last warning was: in that period alone I suffered no less than five operations on that eye. All these were under general anaesthetic, including two in one particularly black period of three days. The problem was that, as sometimes happens in difficult cases, the earlier operations were found to have failed to close all the holes and tears in the retina. This, therefore, had not reattached in its entirety! Indeed, about half the retina detached three times. Worst of all, I could actually *see* all this happening: a traumatic experience indeed! I learned quickly that eyes object more strongly to invasive surgery than virtually all other parts of the human body. Indeed, as I recall this, over two years, and two further operations later, the eye has still not yet entirely settled down.

But my visual problems did not end with my right eye. Not long ago, whilst on a flight from New York to London's Heathrow Airport my left eye began to behave in a now suspiciously familiar way. Gillian and I thanked God this had not happened in the previous three weeks whilst we had been on business, holiday and SGA mission work in the USA. From Heathrow we drove direct to the Bristol Eye Hospital, this time knowing all too well the danger signs! The Casualty Officer who examined my left eye remarked in passing that the thick wadge of notes relating to my right eye were a *"veritable retinal surgeon's Bible"*, being so long and comprehensive a list of retinal surgery procedures and devices! These included laser treatment (three different types!) and cryotherapy (to inflame the inside of the eyeball and make it sticky); hydrocarbon gas and oil bubbles inserted into the main eyeball chamber (to exert pressure on the retina and - hopefully! - reattach it to the now sticky inner surface of the eye); and the use of silicone rubber bands around the outside of the eye (in theory to modify its shape, and provide internal ridges for the retina to grip).

I remarked earlier that eyes are slow to recover from accidents or unnatural interference. Indeed, they are extremely delicate organs, highly susceptible to damage, and very difficult to repair. Today, as a result of the many operations to my right eye, some useful sight has been restored, but the image is distorted, and limited around the edges of my natural field of vision. So I see less, and less well, than I could before. Also, due to the big difference between my two eyes, I have forfeited stereo-vision (that supremely useful ability to see in three dimensions, and so judge depth and distance), and the iris in my right is paralysed, preventing the eye from controlling the amounts of light which enter it.

On the other hand, there are many more things I see which are new! Of these, flashing lights, and small floating bubbles (remnants of the surgical oil not completely removed by the surgeons) are the most remarkable. So far, I am glad to say, my left eye has suffered much less. And we hope it may suffer no more: I need this eye not only for basic tasks such as reading and writing, but even for recognizing other people!

*   *   *   *

So, life has been singularly rough and tough through the last few years. But through all this I have proved, like some other contributors to this book, that God is more than able to sustain us through our faith in Him. For this is not just a 'fair weather faith'. It is also a 'foul weather faith', providing either a haven from the worst storms of life, or a sure way of riding them out with confidence and security.

For myself I can truly say that, as in earlier, happier years, so through all my recent sorrows and difficulties I have been continually conscious of God's love and care. Although I grieved the deaths of my parents, I was saddened by our own loss, not theirs. Because Mother and Father had both been Christians for many years, like the Apostle Paul in the Bible, they *"would prefer to be away from the body and at home with the Lord."* (Paul's Second Letter to the Corinthians, Chapter 5, Verse 8).

Although I and my family hurt desperately as Stella suffered during her illness, we were constantly encouraged by Biblical verses, like the one in the Letter to the Hebrews, Chapter 10, Verse 35, which urges *"Do not throw your confidence (in God) away: it will be richly rewarded",* and in some related respects it already has.

And, although I have found my eye problems traumatic and testing in the extreme, I have been deeply conscious of God's presence with me through them all. He has helped secure for me better vision than many of the doctors expected, for at least some believed my right eye was beyond repair! Let me note just two things which have convinced me of answers to prayer in this regard. During the prolonged course of treatment to my right eye I suffered many post-operative complications. Perhaps the most serious of these followed the most recent operation, to remove the silicone oil which had remained in the eye for over seven months to put and to keep the retina in place. Probably because the pressure in the eyeball dropped too low during and immediately after the operation to remove the oil, the retina suffered what was described to me as a 'gross oedema'. That is to say, the several layers of the retina expanded; indeed, they did so to such a degree that my Consultant thought the tissue would not recover. However, slowly but surely it has done so, restoring useful vision, in answer to the prayers of many good friends around the world! More recently, another surgeon, inspecting the eye for the first time, and bearing in mind all that it had suffered, described the overall results as *"Brilliant!"* My own optician has spoken with admiration of the *"eye having been saved"*! Damaged it certainly has been, but lost it certainly is not!

> *            *            *            *

Now I have always believed that we all do well to *learn from experience*: not only our own experiences, but those of others too. It has always seemed to me that life would be better for everyone if we reacted more sensibly than is commonplace, both to obvious mistakes, and to positive opportunities. Even in the realms of Science there have been many times when we have not reacted sensibly to the findings of others. 'Reinvention of the wheel' may be educational, but it is little more! However, in our personal lives it seems that to 'make our own mistakes' is something we all seem to find irresistible, at least in some stages of our lives, and in some kinds of situations!

As I reflect on all these things, I recognise that one of the greatest pleasures I have had in recent years has been to talk with highly-intelligent, well-trained, imaginative people, not only about their scientific work but, much more inspiringly, about their personal beliefs: the principles they have come to live by, their aims and motives in life, and their sources of 'inner strength', especially when life is hard. This book is one result of some of these discussions. It amply illustrates that Christianity is very much a living faith today, not only *satisfying the intellect*, but, much more basically and importantly, *saving the soul*.

Some final insights into how and why the Christian faith makes these things possible, and how individuals can enter into their own personal relationships with God, can be gleaned from those experiences I have described involving my right eye. There are several questions and answers we can consider in this regard:

FIRST QUESTION: *"Why did the retina detach initially?"*

ANSWER: For many months the experts were not sure. Perhaps earlier surgery to cure cataract of the lens had been responsible; or perhaps some blow to the eye; or perhaps heredity. It was only when the second eye showed signs of similar problems that the *genetic* explanation was confirmed: unfortunately, I had been born with the propensity for such defects to develop.

SECOND QUESTION: *"What happens in such a case if the eye is left untreated?"*

ANSWER: Sight is lost: the eye goes blind. Had I delayed my visit to the optician only a few more days as that giant retinal tear was developing, the eye would have quickly become non-functional. To all practical intents and purposes it would have been dead!

THIRD QUESTION: *"Can eyes affected in these ways be saved?"*

ANSWER: Yes, but only through the help of an expert! And I soon learnt that, within the field of eye surgery as a whole, retinal surgery is a very particular specialism, practiced only by a few.

FOURTH QUESTION: *"Is recovery of eyesight after surgery rapid and complete?"*

ANSWER: Yes, and no! Immediate improvement often occurs, followed by a longer period of slower change, as the eye settles, and the brain helps compensate for more intransigent effects of the earlier disease. But even in the most successful cases, in which difficulties are diagnosed and treated early, some visual damage usually remains.

FIFTH QUESTION: *"How does all this illustrate the Christian message to the world?"*

ANSWER: In the Biblical Gospels, it is reported on several occasions that Jesus gave new sight to the blind. There, and elsewhere in the New Testament, blindness is used as a picture of the spiritual state of people separated from God by sin: people

who have neglected or rejected God, who have lived lives
ignoring Him and His laws, and people who have lacked
proper love and regard for others.

The Bible says that, *by nature*, we all sin in one or more of
those ways: just as I inherited weaknesses in my eyes which
made them prone to disease, so we are all born with the
propensity for the disease of sin. Indeed, sin is much the
worse problem, for we are *all* affected by its consequence, *as
soon as we are born*! Not surprisingly, as with my retinal
problems, the Bible warns that if our sin is untreated we may
soon reach the point beyond which a cure may become
impossible. And if we die with our sins against God
unforgiven, we will have no chance of seeing and enjoying
Heaven. How can we possibly expect to be admitted to God's
home in the life to come if we have never acknowledged Him
as Lord of everything in this present life, and behaved
accordingly?

Now this is all BAD news! But the gospel can be defined as
'God's GOOD NEWS to us all'! Wonderfully, the Bible
explains that God will, as it were, heal our spiritual blindness,
if we ask Him to! He is the only One able to do this, for He is
the One who designed and made us. He is the One who
therefore knows and understands both our sin problem, and
how to cure it. As remarked in an earlier chapter, one of the
many Biblical descriptions of God is as 'the Great Physician'.
While He lived here as the God-man, Jesus Christ, He
showed His love for us more clearly than He had ever done
before. We noted earlier that, on more than one occasion,
Jesus performed the miracle of curing *physical* blindness:
something modern medicine can sometimes do today. But
no-one other than God Himself can cure *spiritual* blindness,
and so enable us to see Himself, ourselves, and others in new,
true, and wonderful ways.

Not only I, but all the folk featured in this book, have had, as it were,
our spiritual sight restored through faith in God. In some cases (like
mine!) this took place whilst we were young; in other cases it did not
happen until later, even much later, in some people's lives. However,
all of us have been delighted with the results! Read again how each of
us has benefited from finding and trusting Him. Some common

benefits will become clear, as well as some which have been more or less unique to the individuals concerned. Similar kinds of benefits could be yours, too, if you will also seek out God.

But a warning is necessary too. Note that, as with my right eye, delaying expert help spells real danger: the longer we ignore our spiritually sick condition, and God's offers of help, the higher the risk that our problem will become 'terminal' - beyond help, incurable. Note, too, that the longer any of us delays seeking His cure, the more the effects of our sin will continue to damage our lives, even if we do eventually decide to come to Him. God promises to forgive and heal us any time we turn to Him, truly regretting our earlier waywardness. He then begins to heal our souls, and prepare us for eternity with Him in Heaven. But in the meantime God does not promise to remove all the temporal consequences of our sins. As in my eyes after surgery, scars will remain in our lives, and in our relationships with others. We should not be surprised by this, for there will often be continuing consequences of sin which involve not only we ourselves but maybe many other people too.

From the testimonies of everyone featured in this book it should be clear that God is real, and that we need His help if we are to fulfil the purposes for which He gave us life. It should be clear, too, that Jesus Christ came to Earth to make it possible for us, individually, to find God and enjoy His care and love for ever afterwards. Unfortunately it is often difficult to see these truths, for sin blinds us to them, and Satan seeks to blindfold folk in every nation and generation. I thank God that He helped doctors save much of the sight of my eyes - but I thank Him much more that He has given me a kind of sight I did not have before I found Him for myself. I spoke earlier of many of the *memorable moments* in my life. None has been as memorable as the evening I first realised I needed God's forgiveness! I spoke earlier of things which have given me *great personal pleasure*. None has given me as great a thrill as knowing and experiencing His friendship and help from day to day!

So, here is one final question: Will *you* learn from all those of us who have shared our personal stories in this book? You see, *you too, can find God* - the greatest discovery anyone can ever make! Ask Him to cure you of spiritual blindness, and you will then see Him yourself, with the 'eye of faith'. Wholly new fields of view, new dimensions, and new experiences will then open up, many with characteristics and qualities you never used to know existed.

The Bible says that, in Christ, *"are hidden all the treasures of wisdom and knowledge."* (Paul's Letter to the Colossians, Chapter 2, Verse 3).

FIND GOD, and all other discoveries will make *more sense* than before.

FIND GOD, and all other discoveries will seem *much less important* than they did before.

FIND GOD, and He will lead you into new areas of truth and experience *beyond any you ever imagined* before.

FIND GOD, and you will want to *share this supreme discovery* with others too!

# APPENDICES

## 1.   THE SLAVIC GOSPEL ASSOCIATION

SGA is a global, non-denominational, evangelical missionary society, founded in 1934 by Peter Deyneka, a Russian emigrant with a deep concern for the spiritual well-being of his compatriots wherever they were to be found.   After the fall of the Iron Curtain, profound political and economic changes spread across the former Soviet Union (most of which now forms the 'Commonwealth of Independent States' or CIS) and Central and Eastern Europe.   Today's SGA ministries are concentrated in these regions, with the aim of better equipping the local, indigenous churches to bring the Gospel of Jesus Christ to their own peoples.   Through a unified strategy, SGA ministries in Australia, Canada, France, Germany, New Zealand, the United Kingdom and the USA work together to that end.   Within this strategy the UK Office concentrates its work of Bible-based training and equipping towards Central and Eastern Europe, whilst other Offices direct ministries into the CIS.

Special mention may be made of media ministries (particularly literature, radio and TV) based increasingly within the target countries themselves; training of nationals for pastoral ministries and church leadership; in-country evangelism; church planting and sponsorship of church planters; conferences and youth camps; children's work; care of the sick and elderly; prison visiting; and provision of medical supplies to hospitals and orphanages.   Six Regional Ministry Centers are maintained in the CIS to support the outreach of national churches, in Moscow, Omsk and Khabarovsk (Russia), Minsk (Belarus), Kiev (Ukraine) and Almaty (Kazakhstan).   Simultaneously, equipping and supporting ministries are taking place in Poland, the Czech and Slovak Republics, Hungary, Romania, Moldova, Bulgaria, Croatia, Serbia and Macedonia.

## 2.   THE RADIO ACADEMY OF SCIENCE

RADAS was designed by the Editor of this book in 1977 at the request of the then President of SGA, Peter Deyneka Jnr., as one of several new radio programmes intended primarily for broadcasting into the USSR under SGA's *"Heaven and Earth"* network designed to strengthen the church in the USSR, and share the Gospel with Believers and Non-believers in their own homes.   A companion programme for children was developed later under the title *"Nature World"*.   RADAS was transmitted several times every week from 1980 through 1992 from major Christian short wave radio stations in Europe, South America, the Far East and elsewhere, not only in Russian, but in other major world languages also.   More recently, transmissions have been from stations within the reception area countries themselves, including Russia and Ukraine.

Excerpts from RADAS programmes have been published regularly in Christian magazines, and related audiovisuals have also been prepared.   In 1984, a collection of testimonies from the earlier RADAS scripts was published by Moody Press in collaboration with SGA entitled *"Scientists Who Believe"*.   Still in print today, the original American version has been reprinted 10 times.   The book has also been translated into several different languages including Chinese, German, Japanese, Mongolian and Serbian.   This new volume, *"Scientists Who Find God"*, has been prepared from scripts written by the present Editor, initially at the request of *"Word of Life Ministries, Inc."* in Tokyo, Japan.   The Japanese version was first published by them in 1996.   A Russian version is now being planned by SGA.

## 3.   SOME USEFUL ADDRESSES

If you would like to learn more about the Slavic Gospel Association and its many ministries, address your letters to the SGA as follows:

UK:     37A The Goffs, Eastbourne, East Sussex BN21 1HF.
USA:   6151 Commonwealth Drive, Loves Park, Illinois 61111.

Or write to one of the following addresses:

Australia:     SGA, P.O. Box 396, Noble Park, Victoria 3174.
Canada:        SGA, Box 250, Streetsville Postal Station, Mississauga, Ontario L5M 2BS.
France:        Association Evangelique Slave, Rue de Mauberge, 59164 Marpent.
Germany:       SGA e.V., Birkenstrasse 2-5, D-63868 Grosswallstadt.

---